122
WAYS TO
BUILD
TEAMS

SECOND EDITION

To my friend Pat Stone, for all the years you kept hiring me to work in your school system, which enabled me to try the information in this book over and over until I got it right.

122
WAYS TO
BUILD
TEAMS

SECOND EDITION

CAROL SCEARCE

FOREWORD BY LAWRENCE W. LEZOTTE

CORWIN PRESS
A SAGE Publications Company
Thousand Oaks, CA 91320

For information:

Corwin Press
A Sage Publications Company
2455 Teller Road
Thousand Oaks, California 91320
www.corwinpress.com

Sage Publications India Pvt. Ltd.
B 1/I 1 Mohan Cooperative
　Industrial Area
Mathura Road, New Delhi 110 044
India

Sage Publications Ltd.
1 Oliver's Yard
55 City Road
London EC1Y 1SP
United Kingdom

Sage Publications Asia-Pacific
　Pte. Ltd.
33 Pekin Street #02-01
Far East Square
Singapore 048763

Printed in the United States of America

Library of Congress Cataloging-in-Publication Data

Scearce, Carol.
122 ways to build teams/Carol Scearce—2nd ed.
　　p. cm.
Originally published as: 100 ways to build teams.
Includes bibliographical references and index.
ISBN 978-1-4129-4458-8 (cloth)
ISBN 978-1-4129-4459-5 (pbk.)
1. Teams in the workplace. I. Scearce, Carol. 100 ways to build teams.
II. Title. III. Title: One hundred twenty two ways to build teams.

HD66.S35 2007
658.4′022—dc22

2006101262

This book is printed on acid-free paper.

07　08　09　10　11　12　10　9　8　7　6　5　4　3　2　1

Acquisitions Editor:	Cathy Hernandez
Editorial Assistant:	Megan Bedell
Copy Editor:	Barbara Coster
Typesetter:	C&M Digitals (P) Ltd.
Indexer:	Pamela Onorato
Cover Designer:	Scott Van Atta
Graphic Designer:	Lisa Miller
Production Artist:	Karine Hovsepian

Contents

Foreword

I f leaders are to succeed in changing the entrenched culture of their organizations, they must have a strategy for planned change. The leaders must take into account the need for changing the norms and beliefs or policies and procedures of the organization. In addition, and at least as important, the leaders need a strategy that will change the way people in that organization behave. Virtually all successful change reduces itself to people change—no small undertaking!

What tools do the leaders have available to create the conditions that will ensure behavioral change in the people who make up an organization? Essentially, the tools that can be used are limited indeed. Some leaders depend heavily on "stick power" to change people. They believe that intimidation, and the threat of punishment, will produce sustained, positive behavioral change. Evidence that stick power is effective is, at best, overstated. Some leaders believe that sustained, positive behavioral change can be achieved by carefully deploying "carrot power"—that if you can create the appropriate rewards and incentives, the desired behavior can be solicited and maintained. The payoff from the careful use of carrot power is a little more positive. But if the carrot power tool is to be used effectively, three conditions must exist. First, the leaders must have an inexhaustible supply of carrots; second, the workers must have an insatiable appetite for carrots; and third, and most important, both the leaders and workers must know precisely what behavior will yield the carrots—no small undertaking!

More enlightened leaders have come to realize that the best hope for creating positive, sustained behavioral change in an organization occurs when the tool of "hug power" is used. According to the noted economist and author Kenneth Boulding, hug power is the power that comes when two or more people connect with each other because of shared beliefs, vision, and values. The resulting synergy represents a very powerful force for sustained positive change. Unfortunately, to unleash the force of hug power means that the people must have the time and opportunity to develop the openness and trust required to discuss beliefs, vision, and values authentically—no small undertaking!

The development of a plan to tap the potential hug power in an organization must start with creating teams of individuals who are willing to risk the openness and trust that are required. Carol Scearce's book represents a valuable source of proven methods and procedures for building effective work teams. These techniques should not be seen as ends in themselves. Rather, these proven practices, as well as the creation of work teams, represent the one best tool we have for changing today's workplace so that it will better serve our society and the society our children will inherit—no small undertaking!

—Lawrence W. Lezotte

Preface

Each year I get many calls from organizations across the country asking for help in establishing teams. I refer them to many excellent sources, including videos, books, and audiotapes. It is not long before they call back saying, "The sources are great, but we have a few problems. First of all, we don't have time to read all the books. Second, we don't really know how to transfer the information to real life." So I find myself packing my suitcase and traveling thousands of miles to offer assistance.

As I reflect on my journeys to these organizations, I find that most of them cannot afford the number of consulting days that it takes to institute quality team building. Their main problem is not in understanding what they read but in how to process the information. I can't tell you how many times someone has said to me, "Carol, if we just had something that would be fun to use and help us process role clarification, how to select a leader, how to celebrate our successes, or any of the other topics you have mentioned, we could do it on our own."

I pondered the problem and decided that maybe an easy-to-use recipe book on the essential areas of teaming would be the answer. That's how *100 Ways to Build Teams* was born.

Fourteen years have passed. I have discovered two additional components that must be added to the original book so that teams will function at a high performing level. Hence the second edition. The two components are agenda design and process tools. I have been amazed and stymied with the lack of understanding when it comes to these two components. I have seldom seen an agenda used in a team meeting that was anything other than a list of topics or ideas to be covered. Most of the time, over half of the topics or ideas were still on the list at the end of the meeting. Sometimes, the list had grown longer due to topics mentioned during the meeting when people went off track and started talking about something else. If a problem arose, I never heard anyone say, "What process should we use to solve our problem?" Instead, I watched as team after team attempted to solve the problem by sitting around and complaining about it and all the things that were wrong with the system or the person who caused the problem. Sometimes someone would throw out a solution that might or might not have been good. No one really knew, because the solution was just yelled out by someone and the team said either yea or nay. Next, someone offered another idea until finally, meeting time was up, so the entire problem and solutions were either tabled or someone said, "Oh, I liked Carl's solution. Let's try that." The meeting was adjourned, and depending on the severity of the problem, it might or might not have been mentioned again.

I spent quite a bit of time interviewing teams and working with teams to find out why these things continued to happen over and over. I found out that administrators and teachers often felt the data they had to use to solve problems were not user friendly, they did not know how to use it, or the data were not easily available to them. It was easier and quicker to use their intuition or their experiences to identify what they believed were root causes. When it came to solutions, the educators I interviewed said they had never come up with solutions any other way than by just brainstorming, selecting from the brainstormed list and hoping implementation would occur because they all agreed on it. There were two main problems with agendas. First, they had never been trained to do any type of agenda format other than list the topic and time. Second, they did not see the value of using an agenda. I never interviewed any administrator or teacher who had used a tool kit of problem-solving processes.

I mention these things not because I want to be pessimistic but because I believe, along with many of the experts such as

Rick DuFour, Art Costa, Larry Lezotte, and Carl Glickman, just to name a few, that collaboration, through teaming, is the best way to initiate and institutionalize school reform. It is through high-performing teams that change has a higher probability of occurring. Teams who are well trained will have the capacity and the intelligence to solve problems and create schools that are high performing.

I spend a lot of time thinking about the two chapters that have been added, taking into account the incredible workload of educators and the amount of time that is left after a full day of work. I have used every activity in the two new chapters many times and have had quite a bit of success. Administrators and teachers have e-mailed me, sent letters, and made comments during meetings that they really liked the tools and found them useful and, in most instances, not complicated. One of the funniest and best comments an administrator made to me was "It took me a month to begin the 10-Step Process. As I worked my way through it, I also learned that if you mess up, you don't die, you just age a few years. Look at me and try to guess how long it took me to get through all 10 Steps. But it made the biggest difference in the implementation of the project. Thanks!" My journey over the last 14 years has taught me so much more than I knew in 1992 about team building. If you liked the first edition of this book, I hope you will find the second edition even more useful. Most of all, I hope you will use the ideas as you work with your team so that you will have success. If your team is successful, your students will be successful. If your students are successful, your school will be successful.

WHO SHOULD USE THIS BOOK?

One of the nice things about this book is that it can be used by anyone who works with people.

- Teachers can use it in cooperative learning.
- Principals can use it for faculty meetings.

- Students can use it for clubs and organizations.
- Superintendents can use it for school boards and other meetings.
- Businesses can use it for meetings.
- Professional organizations can use it for meetings.
- Any type of work team can use it to establish teams.

All you need to do is pick up this book and let it work for you.

WHAT IS THE BEST WAY TO USE THIS BOOK?

I would like to invite you to walk through the different sections with me so that you will become familiar with the book.

Introduction

Each chapter is preceded by a short introduction that explains why the chapter is important. Sometimes I have included stories or examples from my own or others' personal experiences that enhance the meaning of the topic. Feel free to use these stories in your own team training. At times there is additional information from the experts that might help you if someone asks you a question or wants to know more about the topic.

Quotations

Each section has a quotation that captures the essence of the chapter. I have found that quotations have a way of awakening the brain. People love them, and often the quotation is so powerful that you can hear people sigh. It's almost as if they are saying, "Ah, yes, now I understand." My suggestion is that you use the quotation as your opening line to the study of the topic.

Background

Each section has a true story that makes important points about the topic. If you use humor and stories, you make important points and hit on touchy issues more easily. You might want to use humor and stories to introduce the topic or later, when you feel a story would be powerful. One of my stories may spark a memory of something that happened to you that you could share. The key point here is that from the beginning of time, stories have been used to convey powerful messages. Use them!

Did You Know

This section is a list of some important points that the team needs to know. All points come from resources or research that I have collected over the years. I wish they were all original, but they are not. They are a collection from the best minds across the world on teaming. It is these points that build the case for the components included in this book.

From this section you can develop a mini lecture. If you would like to develop a longer lecture, I suggest that you look under the Did You Know sections for all three levels of the topic. For example, each chapter has three levels: Simple Things to Do, Things That Take Effort, and For the Committed. Each level has more facts. You can take all three levels and put together an extensive lecture.

Simple Things to Do

Each topic begins with activities that are simple. This level is designed for teams who are in the "forming" stage. This stage is characterized by excitement, optimism, pride, suspicion, fear, and anxiety. During this stage there is not a high level of trust. Team members don't do business any differently than before. Simple Things to Do will get a team started. If you don't have a lot of time, this is the section for you.

Things That Take Effort

This level is designed to help team members move through the "storming" stage, which is characterized by arguing among members, defensiveness and competition, establishing unrealistic goals, and concern about excessive work. During this stage, members realize something is not right. They aren't really collaborating and functioning as a team. They are beginning to realize that teaming takes effort. This level is for teams who have some time to spend learning about teaming.

For the Committed

This level is designed to help team members move to the "norming" and "performing" stages. In the norming stage, the team has realized that teaming as a way of doing business takes a lot of work. They accept teaming as a way to do things and believe that everything is going to work out. They attempt to gain harmony, they are friendlier, they confide in each other, they share problems, and they have a sense of team cohesion, common spirit, and goals. They are ready to establish and maintain norms. With commitment and hard work, they will move to the performing stage, which is characterized by a better understanding of group processes, better understanding of others' strengths and weaknesses, a high level of trust, and satisfaction at the team's progress. They work through problems and have formed a close attachment to the team.

It is up to your team to decide where they want to begin. My suggestion is to look through the activities on all the levels and select the ones that best suit your team's needs. It could be that you are on one level for one topic and another level for another topic. The beauty of this book is that you can mix and match to suit your needs.

Materials You Will Need

After each activity, the materials you will need are listed. I have seen many an activity fail because the team did not have the materials. Resources are sometimes limited, so I have tried to suggest materials that organizations already have. Most of the activities can be done using only chart paper, colored markers, and masking tape. Please feel free to add any materials you think will make the activity better. There will always be a sample in the directions or an illustration of the handout.

Further Readings

The Further Readings list is not extensive, but the sources listed are excellent. You can get them in most bookstores.

That completes our tour of the book. I hope you found it helpful. Do not limit your potential by using the book only as I have suggested. It is my hope that you will find *122 Ways to Build Teams* user friendly and that it will make your journey into teaming fun, exciting, and successful. Have fun! Teaming is the right thing to do.

Acknowledgments

M y acknowledgments are kind of like winning an academy award. It's not that I have a long list of people to thank; it's that I am so emotional about the people who have helped me. If it had not been for all of them, I would not have written the first or second edition.

My first thanks go to the folks at SkyLight Publications. You were responsible for helping me complete the first edition. Your team encouraged me, walked with me, edited with me, and inspired me to do my best.

For the second edition, my thanks go to Cathy Hernandez at Corwin Press. If you had not called, the second edition would not exist. In fact, if you had not called more than once, it would not exist. You were persistent and encouraging, and I cannot thank you enough because it was you who made me reflect on the last 14 years to see if I had anything significant to add to a second edition.

More than 1,000 thanks go to Lori Smith, my friend from Virginia, who did the typing and the graphics for the new material. Only you know how important you have been to me. You never fail to make me look good, and I can never repay you for the help you have given me. You are a special lady.

Thanks a second time to all the educators across the country who have continued to try out the activities in the first edition. You did them so well and with such gusto. It is because of you that I have such wonderful stories. I admire your courage in trying to change the system.

I would like to thank the reviewers of the first edition. You were encouraging and at the same time you gave me some real food for thought. I have read and reread your comments over and over. Cathy and I discussed them a few times. I have tried to keep all of them in mind while I was rewriting the second edition.

I must thank my husband, David O'Brien. You never complained even though we added a two-year-old to our family last year and you had to do most of the rocking while I did the writing. Thank you so much for supporting every project I have wanted to take on.

Last, but not least, I want to thank Jacob, the latest addition to our family. It is because of you that I want to continue working as hard as I can to help schools be the best that they can be. You are just beginning. I want the best for you.

PUBLISHER'S ACKNOWLEDGMENTS

Corwin Press gratefully acknowledges the contributions of the following individuals:

Steve Hutton, Educational Consultant
Villa Hills, KY

Michelle Kocar, Principal
Avon Heritage South Elementary School, Avon, OH

Kathy Malnar, Superintendent
Hudson Area Schools, Hudson, MI

Gina Segobiano, Superintendent
Harmony-Emge District #175, Belleville, IL

Dana Trevethan, Principal
Turlock High School, Turlock, CA

About the Author

**Carol Scearce** is President of Enlightening Enterprises, a company that provides seminars and workshops to educators. Her most popular workshops are on team building, mentoring, brain research, and research-based teaching strategies. She travels throughout Canada and the United States. Her seminars and workshops are practical, active, and humorous. She models what she preaches and gives participants many opportunities to make connections between the workshop and the real world of school.

She has been in education for over 40 years. After teaching Grades K–8 for a number of years, she received a master's in special education and taught Primary Educable Mentally Retarded for four years. During that time, she received the Outstanding Special Educator of the Year Award. She taught four years at Georgia Southern University and two years at Virginia Commonwealth University. She completed her administration certification and went back to public education, where she was in charge of staff development for a very large school system in Chesterfield County, Virginia. During this time, she was nominated for *Who's Who in Education* and *Who's Who in Staff Development*. She has authored articles and training manuals and has presented at ASCD, NSDC, the Brain Expo, the Council for

Exceptional Children, and Title I Conferences, to name a few. She has conducted over 1,000 workshops with titles such as Team Building, Steps to Organizational Change, Teaching in the High-Performance Classroom, How to Have a Brain-Friendly Staff Meeting, Reading in the Content Areas, Classroom Instruction That Works, and Mentoring the Beginning Teacher.

Introduction

1 *22 Ways to Build Teams* is not a book on theory; it is book that helps nurture and consciously develop the components of team building that are necessary for a high-performing team. However, I would like to look at what experts say about the concept of team building, because it takes time and effort. Teamwork does not happen automatically. Teamwork is also the right thing to do. Richard Elmore (2003), in a study commissioned by the National Governors Association, concluded that

> knowing the right thing to do is the central problem of school improvement. Holding schools accountable for their performance depends on having people in schools with the knowledge, skill, and judgment to make the improvements that will increase student performance.

What Is a "Team"?

Individuals involved in team building need to understand what the word *team* means. It's hard to support something when team members don't have a common understanding. Many people have had past experiences with teams in some way. They can recall, when they were young, being part of a team in Little League or other organized sport, a dance class, a chess team, or a cheerleader team, to name a few. Most people have a sports team they root for throughout the year. I mention this because the concept of teaming is a very familiar one, so naturally people think they know what it is, how to do it, and when to do it. Often they don't want to spend time in training and development because they think it's a waste of time. When I meet a team like this, I ask them to give me their definition of teaming. I have never met a new team where all the members gave me the same definition. They give me parts of the definition, their perceptions, experiences, but never a common definition. Once in a while I meet team members who can give me a definition that is similar, but when asked to explain, their perceptions were different. In reviewing research, I found these thoughts on the word *team:*

- Scholtes, Joiner, and Streibel (2003) say that a team is a group of people who create an environment that supports trust, respect, and collaboration. They have a common understanding of the organization's vision and values and a shared commitment to delighting customers.
- Eaker, DuFour, and Burnette (2002) describe a team as groups of educators who have the benefit of time, focus, parameters, access to information, and ongoing support as they engage in collective inquiry and action research. They work together in an ongoing effort to discover best practices and to expand their professional expertise.
- Roberts & Pruitt (2003) describe a team as a group of people who have expertise necessary for a project and use strategies that are suitable to the task. They are energetic and exert enough effort to complete the task at an acceptable level.
- Martinez (2004) says a team is composed of a group of people, two or more, who are interdependent and are working toward a common purpose.
- Here is a definition, though dated, that captures all of the above, from Francis and Young (1979). They define a team as an energetic group of people who are committed to achieving common objectives, who work well together and enjoy doing so, and who produce high-quality results.

These are but a few definitions of team. The point is that when a school is going to use the team concept, a common definition needs to be developed for the entire group to use as a foundation from which to build their teams. The definition should be clarified so that when statements such as "work well together" are used, everyone on the team knows that working well together means they work interdependently and use tools to gather data. The team has a format for agendas. They have a number of strategies to use when reaching consensus, and they problem solve using processes the team has learned during training. Achieving high-quality results means the team has met its goals and achieved the expected end result. Once a definition has been clarified, it should be so clear that the team could use the definition to evaluate itself.

What Does a Team Look and Sound Like?

Although each team will look different because it is made up of different people, there are specific stages that most teams go through. The stages are *forming, storming, norming,* and *performing* (Tuckman, 1965). By recognizing these stages, team members can better evaluate what they have to do to advance to the highest level of effectiveness.

When a team is *forming,* members are trying to agree upon the purpose and task of the team. They may covertly test the boundaries of acceptable group behavior and may challenge the team's identified leader. During this stage, each person is functioning as an individual rather than a team member. Moving successfully through this stage enables the team to focus on its mission and move toward the performing stage.

Storming is a challenging stage marked by conflict. At this stage, members argue about the task, who's in control, and how the team is going to function. Often members begin to wonder if they want to be on the team because they realize it's going to be a lot of work. During this stage, team members may need help developing a code of conduct, establishing clear leadership, and encouraging collaboration.

In the *norming* stage, the team goes through the steps of team building. Strong leadership has emerged, and members have developed a code of conduct and established clearly defined tasks. Team members understand their roles and know how decisions will be made. They have reconciled competing

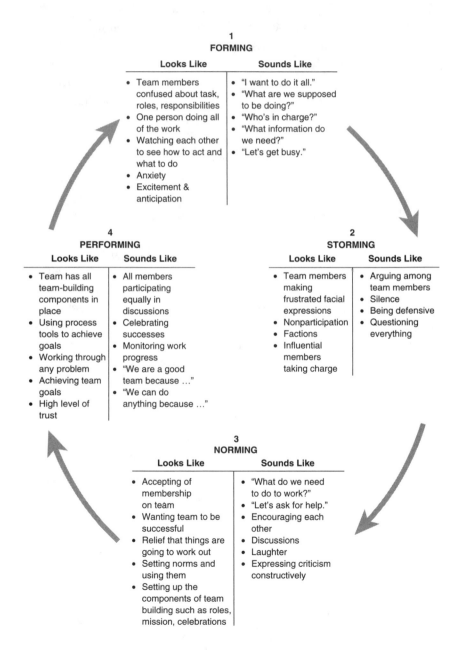

1
FORMING

Looks Like	Sounds Like
• Team members confused about task, roles, responsibilities • One person doing all of the work • Watching each other to see how to act and what to do • Anxiety • Excitement & anticipation	• "I want to do it all." • "What are we supposed to be doing?" • "Who's in charge?" • "What information do we need?" • "Let's get busy."

4
PERFORMING

Looks Like	Sounds Like
• Team has all team-building components in place • Using process tools to achieve goals • Working through any problem • Achieving team goals • High level of trust	• All members participating equally in discussions • Celebrating successes • Monitoring work progress • "We are a good team because ..." • "We can do anything because ..."

2
STORMING

Looks Like	Sounds Like
• Team members making frustrated facial expressions • Nonparticipation • Factions • Influential members taking charge	• Arguing among team members • Silence • Being defensive • Questioning everything

3
NORMING

Looks Like	Sounds Like
• Accepting of membership on team • Wanting team to be successful • Relief that things are going to work out • Setting norms and using them • Setting up the components of team building such as roles, mission, celebrations	• "What do we need to do to work?" • "Let's ask for help." • Encouraging each other • Discussions • Laughter • Expressing criticism constructively

loyalties and responsibilities, know they can work together, and are beginning to make significant progress.

A *performing* team knows how to diagnose and solve problems. Team members are effective and cohesive. They get a lot of work done and achieve high-quality results.

There are no time frames for how long a team stays in a stage or moves to a new stage. A team may cycle through the stages many times, particularly if there is a change in leadership or an influx of new members. The key is to recognize what stage the team is in and act accordingly. The diagram on the previous page helps members recognize what a team looks and sounds like at each stage.

Why Are Teams Important?

Team building is hard work. It takes patience, strong will, knowledge, and courage. It is not for the fainthearted. Before undertaking the task of building high-performing teams, it is important to know why researchers highly recommend using teams to create high-performing schools.

The figure below shows what experts have identified as the "pay value" or benefits of working in teams. I encourage you to share this with staff as they begin their journey toward team building.

"Pay Value" of High-Performing Teams

- Develops a shared vision of what the school could be like
- Promotes cohesion among staff
- Team energy becomes aligned and energizes
- Taps into potential of many minds
- Emphasizes what is important
- Focuses on high-quality results
- Achieves high-quality results
- Higher likelihood of implementation of new ideas
- Higher likelihood of buy-in
- Promotes real-world skills
- Models to students the power of teamwork
- Creates a structure for a professional learning community

What Do Experts Say About Teams?

Most people who love to read professional books are motivated by certain styles, the layout of the book, research, favorite authors, or other factors. I am always inspired by individuals I consider to be experts in the field. For the last 10 or more years, I have read a lot on the subject of team building. I would like to share with you powerful statements by experts on the subject of teams in hopes that it will inspire you to push onward and upward with team building—it's the right thing to do.

The most promising strategy for sustained, substantive school improvement is developing the ability of school personnel to function as professional learning communities.

—R. DuFour & B. Eaker (1998, p. 130)

The Commission recommends that schools be restructured to become genuine learning organizations for both students and teachers; organizations that respect learning, honor teaching, and teach for understanding.

—L. Darling-Hammond (1996)

The ability to collaborate on both a large and small scale is one of the core requisites of post modern society. . . . In short, without collaborative skills and relationships it is not possible to learn and to continue to learn as much as you need in order to be an agent for social improvement.

—M. Fullan (1993)

High school skills needed to succeed in the real world, *"Participates as a member of a team."*

—Secretary's Commission on
Achieving Necessary Skills (1991)

Team building, then, is an important prerequisite to establishing a collaborative learning organization.

—J. Glanz (2006, p. 19)

The success of any school, whether it is striving to meet the requirements of NCLB or some other goal, rests on the ability of the teachers to work with other teachers, administrators, parents, and students.

—M. Martinez (2004, p. 49)

We're pretty happy campers here. We're heavily into the team thing.

—S. Armstrong, Social Studies Teacher, Adlai Stevenson High School (as quoted in Schmoker, 2001)

Team learning is the process of aligning and developing the capacity of a team to create the results its members truly desire.

—P. Senge (1990, p. 236)

1

Trust Building

One Saturday morning, when I was a teenager, a group of friends and I went to Goofy Falls, a beautiful body of water in the interior of Panama. It was during the rainy season, but on this day there was no sign of rain. In fact, the forecast was great! After a morning and afternoon of swimming, I grew tired and decided to take one more jump off the top of the falls. I took my jump and then sat on the rocks below to watch everyone. Suddenly I heard a loud roar. I looked up and saw people at the top of the falls running. Someone yelled, "Get out of the water!" Just as I started to get up, I looked up and saw a wall of water coming over the top of the falls at breakneck speed. I wasn't fast enough. I was swept away in something we had often heard about but never experienced—a dreaded mountain flash flood. The water took me miles down the river, over rocks, under trees—you name it, I think I went over it. For some reason, the water threw me up on a fallen tree. I was able to grab hold. I pulled myself out of the floodwaters and sat shaking and scared to death.

After what seemed like an eternity I heard a voice. I looked up, and standing in the jungle was a young GI with his hand out, beckoning for me to come with him. I had no idea who he was, but something about his face, his eyes, and his voice told me it was okay. It took quite a while to make our way back. Even then we had to be rescued. We were on the wrong side of the falls. The rescue team secured a rope across the rushing water and told me to hang on so they could help me across. I would not budge. Not me! The water was too swift. I felt a hand on my shoulder

> *and heard a voice say, "I'll tie you on my back and carry you across the rope myself." It was the young GI. I immediately stopped crying and did as he said. The onlookers cheered as we safely reached the other side. Why, when I was almost in shock, did I follow someone I didn't know?*

I was too young at the time to understand, but as I reflect back on the young man, I now realize that he radiated confidence when he spoke.

His body and his message were congruent. He had to have had integrity to jump into a flash flood to save someone he didn't know, and he was certainly reliable. These are some of the characteristics of trust.

That's what this chapter is all about. I purposely placed it first in the book because of its importance to the success of the team. Without trust, the team will stay in the storming stage—characterized by difficulties, conflicts, unhealthy confrontation, and so on. Without trust, the team will not move to the performing stage, which is essential in order for the team to do its job.

In Dr. Edwards Deming's Fourteen Points of Management he talks about breaking down barriers between departments. He suggests putting everybody to work to accomplish the transformation of an organization. Teaming is one of the vehicles he suggests to put everyone to work. He talks about the fact that everyone has something to contribute. Without trust, team members will not work together; the team will eventually wither and die.

I recommend that teams begin every meeting with a trust-building activity. When teams are first forming, they need to devote 15 minutes of the first 10 meetings to trust building. As they move to the norming stage (characterized by an attempt to achieve harmony, friendliness, a sense of team cohesion, and establishing team ground rules) and the performing stage (characterized by constructive self-change, close attachment to the team, and high productivity), they can cut the trust-building time down to 5 to 10 minutes per meeting.

Simple Things to Do: Trust Me, the Check Is in the Mail

It is better to suffer wrong than to do it, and happier to be sometimes cheated than not to trust.

—Dr. Samuel Johnson

Background

I find that people are full of uninformed optimism when they first work together. They want to skip the trust-building section and get on to the task at hand. To do so is a big mistake. While designing a program for a middle school, I asked the principal how much work the staff needed to do to build trust. He assured me that the members of his staff cared for each other, worked well together, and were ready for the high-level teaming skills. "Skip the touchy-feely stuff!" he said. I did, and I must tell you it was the worst training day of my life. They "niced" each other to death over the roles, they reluctantly shared ideas, and they wouldn't share ideas with other teams. Some didn't talk at all, some actually admitted to me they did not like their team, and two or three kept saying in a small voice, "We're new here . . . what's going on?" I went back to my hotel room and did what Madeline Hunter calls "monitoring and adjusting." What these teachers needed was the first level of trust building. They needed to start out with simple, nonthreatening activities.

Did You Know

- People use communication barriers such as criticism, name-calling, threatening, and moralizing over 90 percent of the time when dealing with a problem or a need to be fulfilled.
- The most common cause of team failure is the inability of team members to get along; that is, there's no trust.
- People often think trust is automatically built into their team because they are committed and have good will.

#1. Trust Talk

Ask each team member to think of a person he or she really trusts.

It can be someone in his or her personal or professional life. Allow one minute for each team member to think. Then ask them to share with the group three characteristics the person has that makes him or her trustworthy. Go around the group and ask each person to share his or her characteristics as the recorder writes them on a chart. Then lead the group in a discussion about how the team might use these characteristics to develop trust. As the team makes suggestions, the recorder lists them on another piece of chart paper. Tape the list on the wall so the team can refer to the ideas every now and then to see how they are doing.

Materials You Will Need

2 pieces of chart paper

masking tape

colored markers

#2. You're On

Tell the group that you will ask each team member to talk about himself or herself for three minutes. They may talk about family, profession, hobbies, or anything else that will help the team know them better. Give them a minute to think of what they are going to say. When the minute is up, ask everyone to get a piece of paper and a pencil. As each team member shares, any member who has a question jots it down so he or she can ask the person after all the team members have shared. Ask someone to begin. After three minutes, call time and move on to the next person. When everyone has had a turn, open up the floor and allow anyone to ask questions or discuss information they found interesting. When everyone has asked all their questions, ask how this activity has helped team members get to know each other better.

Materials You Will Need

a piece of paper and a pencil for each team member

#3. Feeling Groovy

Ask each team member to list on a piece of paper three things that could happen so that at the end of the team meetings he or she could walk away and say, "Wow, I enjoyed working with my team today. It was great!" Examples might be humor, support for ideas, and being treated with respect. Allow one or two minutes for the team to write, then call on one team member at a time. Ask each member to share his or her thoughts and clarify when needed. The recorder writes the responses on a chart. Tape the chart on the wall and refer to it from time to time to check on how the needs of the group are being met.

Materials You Will Need

a piece of paper and a pencil for each team member

1–2 pieces of chart paper

masking tape

a colored marker

#4. T-Shirt Art

Tell the team members they are going to spend some time talking about themselves. Suggestions for sharing are books they like, favorite TV programs, what they like best about their jobs, what motivates them to work, and what characteristics they have that will make them a valuable team member. Then give the team a large sheet of chart paper and colored magic markers. Have them cut a large T-shirt out of the chart paper. Then ask them to design a logo with a slogan on it that represents their team. For example, if they see themselves as caring, they could adopt the bear as their logo and use the slogan "Because We Care!" Another team may see themselves as caring and have five sombreros as their symbol with the slogan "Five Amigos Working Toward Transformation."

Materials You Will Need

> chart paper
>
> colored markers
>
> scissors

#5. Business Cards

This activity is a great one to do after the team has met a couple of times and knows each other better. Tell team members that they have spent a great deal of time getting to know and understand each other. Tell them that as a team they are going to design a business card that represents them and what they stand for. They will have it printed and share it with other staff. For example, a team with a Care Bear logo might design a business card with bear paws on it. The card might contain the members' names and a sentence that reads, "Call 1-800-WE-CARE if you need help and support." Each team puts its cards into a large fishbowl. From time to time the administrator pulls a card and does something special for that team.

Materials You Will Need

> a piece of poster board or chart paper
>
> assorted colored markers
>
> printed business cards

#6. The Name Game

Ask the team members to come up with three self-descriptive words that start with the first letter of their first name. For example, Carol might use the words *caring, comical,* and *committed* to describe herself to her team. The recorder writes the descriptors on a chart. Lead the team in a discussion about how these characteristics of team members will make them a powerful team.

Materials You Will Need

a piece of chart paper

a colored marker

THINGS THAT TAKE EFFORT: YOU CAN DEPEND ON ME

I wish I had some way to make a bridge from man to man. . . . Man is all we've got.

—Cross Daman in Richard Wright's *Outsider*

Background

Not long ago I was in New York just beginning a workshop. I had my attention grabber ready. Just as I was about to begin, a young man in the workshop walked up and said, "Hi, you and I have a mutual friend." I smiled at him and asked who it was. He then told me something I had told our mutual friend in confidence. When he finished, he said, "She told me you wouldn't mind her sharing with me because you were a very open person." I was so stunned and offended. All morning I was very uncomfortable. I ended up having dinner with the young man and lunch the next day. It wasn't until the last day of the workshop that I began to feel comfortable with him.

We spent some time getting to know each other, during which we established a friendship. We progressed to a new level of trust, but I must admit it took some effort. Trust among colleagues is very much like that. Trust builds gradually, incrementally, and with effort. As the team matures, the level of trust increases. The members no longer feel a need to hide their feelings. They begin to level with each other and let their guard down. Members believe they can reveal aspects of themselves and their work without fear of being judged by team members.

Did You Know

- Trust influences all aspects of human interaction.
- Trust will develop over time if the team is moving in positive directions. Trust will increase or decrease, depending on how the members react to each other.
- As trust builds, members are open to learning from each other.
- Team members who laugh and take risks together build trust at a faster rate and on a higher level than if they do not.

#7. Secrets

Ask the members to divulge something they have never told about themselves. An example might be something that happened their first year on the job or a negative opinion they formed about someone that turned out to be wrong. When everyone has had a turn, tell the team not to be misled into thinking this is an easy activity. It takes quite a bit of trust to reveal mistakes.

Materials You Will Need

#8. Sharing Time

Ask team members to bring a special artifact to the team meeting. It should be something that is really meaningful to them. For example, one member might bring a picture of his or her grandparents. Another member might bring a baby shoe. They are to explain what it means to them and why it is important. Explain to the team that these things help them get to know each other better. Tell the team that trust is built through sharing parts of ourselves with others.

Materials You Will Need

artifacts from each person

#9. Trust Creature

Ask the team to share the reasons they trust each other. On a chart, list attributes of their team that indicate trust. Tell them that as a team they will create a creature that represents the attributes they listed. Have them hang the Trust Creature in their meeting room. If applicable, have them share their creatures with the other teams.

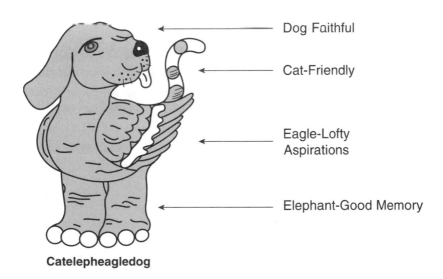

Dog Faithful

Cat-Friendly

Eagle-Lofty Aspirations

Elephant-Good Memory

Catelepheagledog

Materials You Will Need

a piece of chart paper

construction paper

assorted colored markers

scissors

glue

masking tape

#10. Human Trust Check

List and discuss the following trust factor descriptors on a chart:

We listen to each other.

We are sensitive to body language.

Our team climate brings out the best in all of us.

We are comfortable with disagreement.

All voices are given equal power.

We feel safe and validated in our interactions.

We are an interdependent team.

Construct a human trust graph on the wall by placing three signs spaced about five feet apart. The signs should read, from left to right, HIGH, MEDIUM, and LOW. Tell team members they will rate their perception of the trust level of the team by standing under the sign that best represents their feelings about the trust level in the group. If team members read the trust factors on the board and rate all of them a 4 or a 5, then they would stand under the HIGH. If they would rate the trust factors mostly 3's with one or two 4's, they would stand under MEDIUM. If they rate the trust factors all 1's and 2's, they would stand under LOW. Ask the resulting groupings to discuss among themselves why they feel the way they do about the trust level of the team. Tell them that after they have a few minutes to discuss, a person they select will share their grouping's thoughts with the whole team. Call the entire team back together and ask each representative to share his or her group's thoughts. Keep in mind that a team that is just forming may score in the LOW range because the members do not know each other. The team brainstorms ways to help overcome any low and medium concerns. The recorder writes down the solutions, and the team members check themselves as to how they are doing at every team meeting until the trust level from each member is in the HIGH range.

Materials You Will Need

3 large cards labeled HIGH, MEDIUM, and LOW

list of trust factors

3 pieces of chart paper

3 colored markers

FOR THE COMMITTED: PEOPLE WHO NEED PEOPLE ARE THE LUCKIEST PEOPLE

Everyone has a vast capacity for being more understanding, respectful, warm, genuine, open, direct, and concrete in his human relationships.

—George Gazda, educator

Background

I was a little nervous as I began the workshop at Townline Elementary School. I had worked with the group before and had planned some sophisticated activities. I gave the first set of directions and watched as the wild rumpus began. I was the observer and was to record their behaviors. Words cannot express how these people worked together. I'm not sure I've ever seen a staff like this. They were so open, full of fun, honest, supportive, and I could use at least 10 other adjectives. If people made mistakes, it was no big deal and they would try something else. The great thing was that if I hadn't known who the principal was, I wouldn't have been able to pick him out of the group during this activity. He was one of them. What was it? What was making this staff appear to be different? It wasn't that they had mastered all the teaming skills. In fact, they had a hard time reaching consensus. It seemed as if they had no written norms of behavior for teamwork, and they all talked at once. They still had a lot of room for improvement. All of a sudden it dawned on me—they trusted each other. I mean absolutely and completely. They felt totally free to be who they really were. I have to say it was a joy to watch. My nervousness disappeared, and when they voted to adopt me, I came willingly into the Townline family.

Did You Know

- The leader of the team must always monitor the level of trust closely, for without trust the team will not continue to function effectively.
- Authenticity is the key element of trust.
- Trust develops from adequate or total information so that individuals can influence or make decisions and control their own work.

#11. Burst Write

Ask each team member to write a one-page paper on the importance of trust on a team. Their papers should talk about essential characteristics team members must exhibit, what would cause them not to trust, and so on. Tell them to use the Burst Write technique wherein they write for five minutes without stopping or editing. Give them one week to complete the paper. At the next team meeting, ask the members to share their thoughts. Label three pieces of chart paper as follows: Importance of Trust, Essential Characteristics, and Behaviors

That Cause Low Trust. Record what the members share. Lead the team in a discussion of things they can consciously and systematically do to encourage a high level of trust. Together, design a plan that includes activities that reinforce trust.

Materials You Will Need

a piece of paper and a pencil for each team member

3 pieces of chart paper

masking tape

a colored marker

#12. Wonderful Me

Distribute the Wonderful Me handout. (See the example of a completed handout below.)

Tell the team members that as they think about the images they have of themselves, they are to work quickly and record

---

WONDERFUL ME

List 5–6 words that describe you.

- Friendly
- Full of energy
- Many moods
- Adds flavor

What kind of animal best describes you?
What musical instrument best describes you?
What food best describes you?

Animal	Musical Instrument	Food
HORSE	VIOLIN	CILANTRO
Why:	**Why:**	**Why:**
• Friendly	• Many moods	• Adds flavor to
• Full of energy		a dish

their first thoughts. Once they finish, they go to the WHY section of each box and list reasons they are like the animal, the instrument, and the food they chose to describe themselves. In other words, if a member described herself as a horse, she should describe why she is like a horse.

Make a chart using the model below. Have the team members share what they have written on their worksheet. Write down what they say on the chart.

Discuss what each team member gained or achieved through this activity.

Team Member	Animal	Instrument	Food	Words
Jeff	Horse	Violin	Cilantro	Friendly Full of energy Many moods Adds flavor

Discuss how this process reinforces a high level of trust.

Materials You Will Need

a copy of the Wonderful Me handout for each team member

a large chart for gathering responses

colored markers

masking tape

2

Mission Making

Charles Garfield, in his book Peak Performers, tells the story of a senior vice president of an aerospace company who couldn't understand the high motivation level of some of his employees who had such mechanical and repetitive jobs. He acknowledged that the group's job was essential to the success of the plant. In fact, if they didn't do their job well, it could mean extensive damage to the plant. Garfield's curiosity was piqued. When he visited the department, he noticed that all the workers wore green surgical smocks. "Oh, you noticed," the foreman said. "I got them from my son. He's a cardiovascular surgeon, and he got them so I could give them to the gang. We wear them because we are surgeons, just like my son. He takes care of pipes in the body and we take care of pipes in this plant. It isn't going to have any breakdowns as long as we're working on its arteries." Stenciled on the workers' locker doors was "DR." Their mission statement was "Take care of these pipes the way a doctor takes care of your heart." Their mission motivated them to those high levels of commitment and performance.

This story illustrates so well the importance of a team's mission. The mission should clearly define what the team cares about and wants to accomplish. It is through the mission that team members become committed. Mission statements empower people and lead them to action. Missions enable teams to concentrate on what is important, collaborate on how they are going to carry out the mission, set quality standards, and communicate what the organization stands for.

The mission statement should embody the answers to these questions:

1. Who will deliver the service?

2. Who will benefit?

3. What is the nature of the service?

4. What constitutes observable evidence?

5. What is the level of accountability?

The mission becomes a basis of resource allocation, which could be time, money, or people. The team should discuss and evaluate the mission on a regular basis. The mission is the basis of measurable goals and team outcomes. The team can refer to it when important decisions are made. It becomes the driving force of the team.

This chapter is near the beginning of the book because of its importance to the success of team building. The mission should be intact when the team is being formed.

SIMPLE THINGS TO DO: UP, UP, AND AWAY

Vision setting is the domain of leaders.

—Monte Moses

Background

"I really don't know why I'm here."

"I was told to attend!"

"I was absent the day I was selected."

"Our school voted to go to the teaming concept. That's all I know."

"I'm representing my company's improvement team. We're going to be doing some things together, so I'm here to learn how."

Do these statements sound familiar? In most of the workshops I conduct on teaming, about three-fourths to one-half of the participants don't have a clear picture of their mission. These participants usually want me to tell them what their mission is! I've always wondered why they think *I* would know if *they* don't know. My guess is that because humans are teleological by nature, meaning "we seek out and move toward that which we can picture," we are desperate for a clear mission. In order to be committed to an idea, we have to know what we're being asked to commit to!

Did You Know

- It is a leader's job to get people thinking along the same lines.
- The leader's role in planning is to share his or her vision and then empower as many people as possible whose contributions will ensure successful planning.
- The leader needs to create a shared image of what the team can become.
- Teams need a vision of greatness that can propel them to unprecedented levels of performance.

#13. Keep It Simple

This process for writing a mission is the simplest method. It is quick, and will suffice for some teams. Place a large piece of paper on the wall with the following statement:

The major reasons for the development of this team are to achieve the following:

Spend some time discussing the reasons with the team and list the responses on a chart. Then ask the team to synthesize its thoughts into three or four sentences. You may want to have them do Activity #19 first to generate a list of values and then see how many of them are represented in the team mission. For example, if one of their shared values is learning from colleagues, they should see that through the teaming effort, they will have the opportunity to do so. This may be the first time they have taken the time to talk about what they value! If the team has similar values, then their teaming mission will most likely be successful.

Materials You Will Need

1 piece of chart paper

a colored marker

masking tape

#14. Let's Get Graphic

Give each team a large sheet of paper and five markers of assorted colors. Tell them to spend 15 minutes discussing why they are using the teaming approach. They then must represent their thoughts with a graphic organizer, a visual representation of their discussion. An example would be a school that is moving to the middle school concept. Let's say the team discusses ideas such as (a) many heads are better than one, (b) students become real when all of us focus on them, (c) we can learn from each other, and (d) our mission is to serve each student more effectively. The team would then look at all their comments and thoughts and create a picture that symbolizes their discussion. Allow 30 minutes for the team to complete the graphic organizer. If a number of teams are doing this activity, then they can share their graphic organizers with each other.

Materials You Will Need

chart paper

assorted colored markers

masking tape

#15. Let's Use Our Senses

Give the team a large piece of paper and instruct the members to draw an eye in one column, an ear in the second column, and a heart in the third column.

Ask them to discuss the mission of the team as they perceive it. They are to list concrete behaviors under the three columns, behaviors that would be occurring if everyone understood the mission of the team. Give examples to make sure the team understands the task. For example, you might tell the team that under "Looks Like," they might write, "People working collaboratively." Under "Sounds Like," they might write, "It's nice not to have to solve all my problems alone." Under "Feels Like," they might write "A sense of belongingness." If a number of teams are doing this activity, they might share their charts with other teams.

Materials You Will Need

chart paper

colored markers

masking tape

#16. A Penny for Your Thoughts

Ask each team member to get out a sheet of paper and be ready to work individually. Tell the team members that you are going to ask them to think about something they are very familiar with, have touched hundreds of times, have thrown away, have wished for, have thought was worthless, and have been counting since they were two years old. Tell them the object is a penny. They are to individually list as many attributes of a penny as they can remember. After about five minutes, ask them to get with their entire team and see if they can find at least 19 attributes. Give them about eight minutes to create the list. Give each team a penny and let them check their list. When they're finished, lead them in a discussion about what they learned about working alone versus working with a team. How does this relate to working together as a team with a common mission?

Materials You Will Need

a piece of paper and a pencil per person

a piece of chart paper and a colored marker per team

pennies

#17. What's a Team to Do?

Ask each team member to draw a web on a piece of paper. Use the web model in the illustration below. Have them list words on their individual webs that describe their perception of their team's mission. Allow five minutes for individuals to complete their webs. Then have everyone share their responses and create a new team web that has all of their perceptions on one piece of paper. Then lead them in a discussion about the mission of the team.

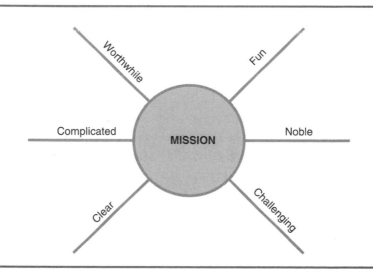

Materials You Will Need

a piece of paper and a pencil per team member

a piece of chart paper and a colored marker per team

Things That Take Effort:
Let's Do It Together

A mission is worthless unless it's put to work.

—George Patterson

Background

I noticed that when I mentioned the word *mission* to a group of educators, they groaned. I was curious and asked what the problem was. They admitted they had a mission, but that it had been a pain. They said their mission statement was about four or five sentences long. They knew it was okay because they had called their colleagues at other schools to compare mission statements. One member said, "Since they all look alike, why not have a mission swapping party, take the best from all, and sell it to anyone needing a mission?" That comment brought laughter from the group.

One of the reasons many people don't get excited about drafting a mission statement is that no one has ever taught them the process. Unfortunately, many of us have not been encouraged to take risks. We have not been told that failure is not fatal. No one wants to admit they don't know how to do something. People sometimes suffer through a task just to get it done. There are a number of processes that will help teams develop a mission. Some are more involved than others. The trick is to find the one that best suits your needs and do it. Having a team mission statement is key to the success of a team.

Did You Know

- To succeed in a big way, a team needs to think as one.
- A mission has to be a team thing. Everyone has to buy into it.
- Every team must have a mission. Without a mission, the team will cease to exist.
- Values are basic to all matters of choice and decision.

#18. What Am I Living For?

Explain to the team members that they will use this activity to discuss values. Human beings are value driven; they tend to act on things they value. Put the following questions on a chart:

- What do I want out of my professional life?
- What do I count as personal profit from my job?
- What do I like about my job?
- What do I believe about my job?
- What is my definition of job success?

Ask each team member to take 30 minutes to reflect on responses to the questions. Have them share answers to come up with how they are alike and how they are different. Ask them to write for three minutes (without stopping) about how the values activity relates to their perception of their teaming mission.

Materials You Will Need

a piece of paper and a pencil for each team member

chart paper

a colored marker

#19. Top Five

Top Five is a good way to discuss values, because the examples are there for the team. Give each team member a copy of the following handout:

Top Five

Dedication to student growth

Promoting self-esteem

Belief in evolving abilities

Total development of the student

Dedication to school improvement

Dedication to personal and professional growth

Loyalty to staff and school

Honesty and forthrightness

Cooperative support

Upholding school procedures

Note: If the team is not a school team, modify the Top Five handout to fit the organization. For example, instead of "Dedication to student growth," it could be "Dedication to customer growth." Instead of "Dedication to school improvement," it could be "Dedication to organization or department improvement."

Ask team members to rank order the 10 items according to the ones they value the most, with 1 being the most valued and 10 the least valued. Ask the team members to share their rankings. Once they have shared, place a card with each value on the wall. Have the team vote on each value using the chart on the next page, and try to reach consensus on the top five values of the team. Lead them in a discussion of the importance of understanding what their teammates value and how it relates to their idea of the team's mission.

CONSENSUS CHART

 5 (5 FINGERS) = YOU'RE ALL FOR IT; TOP PRIORITY

 4 (4 FINGERS) = YES; HIGH ON MY LIST

 3 (3 FINGERS) = O.K. WITH ME

 2 (2 FINGERS) = LET'S TALK MORE

 1 (1 FINGER) = WILL TRUST GROUP

 O (FIST) = NO! AN ALTERNATIVE IS _____

Materials You Will Need

a copy of the Top Five handout and a pencil per person

1 set of large index cards with the values from the Top Five handout written on them

1 enlarged copy of the Consensus Chart

masking tape

#20. Why Are We Here?

Invite the team to a mission meeting. Set up the room so that no more than six people are sitting at a table. Distribute a piece of chart paper and a marker to each table. Have them write the following questions at the top of their charts:

- Why does this team exist?
- What is the value added by this team?
- What are the expected outcomes?
- What is the team's overall contribution to the system?

Ask the group to listen to your vision, including the reason for teaming. When you are finished, ask the groups to discuss the questions on the chart and make notes on the chart itself. Walk around to each group and ask if they need more information or clarification of any points you made. Allow 15 to 20 minutes for the groups to respond to the chart questions. While they are working, prepare four charts, each with one of the questions from the list above. For example, one chart will have, "Why does this team exist?" The second chart will have, "What is the value added by this team?" and so on. Tape them to the wall. Ask each team to share the answers they have on their charts. Compile a master list on the appropriate wall charts. Once all teams have shared, have them look at the wall charts and clear up any misconceptions about the mission.

Materials You Will Need

a piece of chart paper and a colored marker per group

4 charts with the questions written on them

masking tape

FOR THE COMMITTED: I BELIEVE

The best kept secret in America today is that people would rather work harder for something they believe in than enjoy a pampered idleness.

—John W. Gardner

Background

During one of my teaming workshops, I mentioned how important it is to have a team mission. A woman raised her hand and with a long face told me her team had a mission but that it didn't seem to make any difference in the quality of the team's work. She said the team didn't ever refer to it. During the break I asked her to tell me the story. It turned out that when three of the teachers on the team suggested they develop a clearly defined mission, the rest of the team told them to go ahead and write something. They would decide if it was okay. The three teachers tackled the task with gusto. They finished the mission and the rest of the team said it was great. Presto—it was adopted. I must say it was well written. In fact, it was quite grand.

What happened in this situation? First, the entire team didn't have ownership. The mission was the effort of a few. Second, even though the mission was well written, it was not based on the values of the team. If the team had done a values audit and correlated their mission with their values, I guarantee they would be walking their talk. It takes commitment to go through the process, but I have found when teams are willing to make that commitment, it is always worth the effort.

Did You Know

- Team members characteristically exhibit a high degree of individualistic behavior due to the many different beliefs, values, and assumptions they make about the purpose of what they are doing.

- The different values and beliefs of team members often lead them to be at odds with one another.
- The team mission should be stated in writing, be clearly understood, be visible to the teams, and guide the team's actions.

#21. Something of Value

Ask team members to pretend that they have a son or daughter who has just accepted a first job. One day they run into an adult who says, "Oh, you're _____'s parents. I work with him [or her]."

Make a list of some of the things you would like this person to say about your son or daughter. Once they complete this list, tell them to get a piece of chart paper and draw two large circles. Label one circle SAME, label the other circle DIFFERENT. Have a discussion about the similarities and differences among team members.

Make the following points. The things they listed can be described as values. When we have children, we spend most of our parent life trying to help our children develop these values. We often don't talk about values, and it is possible for team members to respect each other but be at odds due to differences in values.

Give the team a stack of 4 × 6 cards and some colored markers. Have the team members break up into pairs. Ask each pair to brainstorm for 10 or 15 minutes to generate values that they hold in high esteem concerning their work. Mention to the team that they might want to think of what their work means in today's society, what do they value about leadership, individual difference, community, and so on. This list is not exhaustive; it just gets them thinking.

Each pair is to write each different value on a card. Tell them they can write one to four words on a card. When time is up, each pair shares its cards with the team. Throw out any duplicates from other pairs and tape the rest on the wall.

When all the values are displayed on the wall, give each person five colored stick-on dots. Instruct everyone to move around the room and read all the value cards. They are to vote for the values that are most important to them by sticking a dot on a value card. Individuals may stick all five dots on one card, or three dots on a card and two on another, or any combination they like.

After the voting is finished, throw away any card with no sticker dots. The entire group then should look at the value cards on the wall and place them in groups. For example, cards that have the values of collaboration, shared decision making, teamwork, trust, and communication might be grouped together. Once this step has been completed, the team names the categories. An example might be leadership or collegiality.

Have the team look at the results and discuss what the activity revealed about the values the team members hold in

---

- Why do you value that?
- Is that view consistent with what we know about . . . (work, leadership, etc.)?
- How does this value relate to our view on . . . (work, leadership, etc.)?
- How does this value differ from the way we do business now?
- Is there anything we have left out?

---

high esteem. The next step is for the team to look at their values and discuss the following questions:

Materials You Will Need

5–6 index cards per pair

1 colored marker per pair

masking tape

5 sticker dots per person

#22. We're Mission Bound and Down

Explain that a team mission statement is composed of one to four sentences that answer three questions:

1. What function does the team perform?

2. For whom does the team perform this function?

3. How does the team go about achieving this function?

Place a chart on the wall with this statement on it:

What function does the team perform?

Ask the team members to develop a list of statements that describe the function of the team. For example, a middle school team might list "To discuss as a team any students having problems." A nursing staff team might list "To determine if there is a gap between care goals and what we are actually doing." An automobile quality control team might list "To make our product more appealing to safety-conscious customers."

Once the team members complete this list, have them examine each function statement and decide for whom the function is intended. For example, the function statement "to discuss as a team any students having problems" is for the student and the teachers, so the team would write in the margin "students and teachers."

Place a chart on the wall with this statement on it:

What does the team need to function?

Ask the team to develop statements that define what the team needs in order to function.

When the team members have completed the lists, they are ready to draft their mission statement. They will look at their list and in a comprehensive statement of one to four sentences capture the essence of all the lists. The mission statement must not be so wordy that it is hard to understand or hard to remember.

Materials You Will Need

1 chart titled "What Function Does the Team Perform?"

1 chart titled "What Does the Team Need to Function?"

1 chart for drafting a mission statement

a colored marker

#23. Let's Get Critical

Once the team members write their mission, they may want to take it a step further and identify some critical issues. Use the following handout.

Lead a discussion concerning the critical issues. This discussion may take two or three team meetings. The investment in time is important, because if these issues go unresolved, the

---

Critical Issues

- What changes in the organization's structure are necessary for us to accomplish our team mission?
- What new capabilities and resources will we require?
- What are the implications for current beliefs, policies, and procedures?
- What are the consequences of staying with the way we are doing things now?
- What is the impact of the new way of doing things on our internal and external customers?
- How can we effectively evaluate our new way of doing things?

team may not be able to carry out its mission effectively. Write each issue discussed on a piece of chart paper and record the responses. Have the team members discuss what steps they must take to deal with the critical issues.

Materials You Will Need

a piece of chart paper for each critical issue to be discussed

colored markers

masking tape

3

Discovering Leadership

Have you ever met someone you would call an unforgettable character? One time I was on an airplane and I sat next to a man who told me his life story. He had spent 17 years in a maximum security prison for armed robbery. As he told his story, I learned that he was The Man in prison. Nothing went down without his permission—he literally ran the show. I began to get a little nervous. I glanced down at his feet to see if they were shackled. I just knew he was being transported covertly to another prison. I le noticed my discomfort immediately and smiled. "Are you nervous?" he asked. I giggled like a teenager and lied, "Oh no, why do you say that?" "You look nervous. Don't worry, I'm on the up and up nowadays," he said. The plane landed before he finished his fascinating story. He gave me his business card, and we parted company. End of story? No! Months later I was reading a brochure someone had given me about an outstanding motivational speaker whose fee was $3,000 per day. I flipped the brochure over to look at the picture, and lo and behold, there was my plane mate! I was so stunned I called him up and told him I wanted to hear "the rest of the story." He told me that while in prison, a teacher noticed he had leadership skills. The teacher offered to get him some help if he would accept the responsibility of leadership and use his skills to lead a positive life. He accepted the leadership role with gusto, and the rest is history. Now he is one of the most sought-out motivational speakers in the United States and is considered to be a leader in the area of organizational change.

This individual was willing to make the commitment to developing his leadership skills. He then accepted the responsibility of putting his skills to work in a constructive way. Warren Bennis (1989), in his book *On Becoming a Leader*, makes an important distinction between leaders of people and managers of people. He says, "Leaders are people who do the right thing; managers are people who do things right" (pp. 111–112).

I often see one of three types of leadership emerge on teams. One type occurs when an administrator or other higher-up is on the team. In this case, the team sometimes automatically chooses him or her to lead. I believe this happens because people are afraid to choose someone different. They may be afraid it would hurt the administrator's feelings, or they may be afraid of retribution from the administrator. Maybe they don't believe anyone else can lead. Maybe they don't have enough trust that the administrator would be able to sit back and let someone else have the role.

The second type of leadership I sometimes see is one where "anyone will do as long as it's not me." The team doesn't discuss or really evaluate the type of person they think should be their team leader. No one wants the job, much less has any idea what leadership entails.

The third type of leadership I have seen is the type where one person wants the role because of the status and power. When this person becomes leader, look out! Shared decision making just went out the door. This person's motto is "My way or hit the highway!" He or she often sees this as an opportunity to run the show.

When these types of leadership emerge, the team will continue to function but at a very low level. In fact, one really couldn't call it a team. It becomes a committee.

This chapter will help your team select a leader who will do the right thing. This can happen only if the team members spend time thinking about what leadership should look like for their team to function and if they carefully select their leader or leaders. One thing that makes a team different from a committee is that on a team, leadership can be shared.

In Robert Marzano, Timothy Waters, and Brian McNulty's (2005) book *School Leadership That Works: From Research to Results*, 21 responsibilities of a school leader are listed. They are as follows:

Monitoring/Evaluating

Culture

Ideals/Beliefs

Knowledge of Curriculum, Assessment, and Instruction

Involvement in Curriculum, Assessment, and Instruction

Focus

Order

Affirmation

Intellectual Stimulation

Communication

Input

Relationships

Optimizer

Flexibility

Resources

Contingent Rewards

Situational Awareness

Outreach

Visibility

Discipline

Change Agent

They mention that it would be rare to find a single individual who has the capacity or would be able to master all 21 responsibilities. The authors go on to say that the focus on leadership should shift from one individual to a leadership team. If this were the case, the team membership would comprise all 21 responsibilities.

However, before the team decides to rotate leadership among the team members, it needs to be sure that everyone wants to be a leader and that everyone has some of the 21 leadership responsibilities.

SIMPLE THINGS TO DO:
IT TAKES TWO TO TANGO

All resources are not obvious; great leaders find and develop available talent.

—Dwight D. Eisenhower

Background

One fine spring morning I stopped in to see one of my favorite middle school principals just to say hello. I noticed he looked kind of down in the dumps. I asked him what was wrong, and he began to tell me that he was losing many of his "best" staff members to the new middle school that was opening in the fall. I tried to offer words of encouragement, but secretly I thought, "Poor guy. The school won't be the same."

When I saw him again in the fall, he was smiling! I said, "Things must have changed—the teachers didn't transfer?" He looked at me and said, "Carol, it was amazing. Once those teachers left, I told the staff we were going to have to pull together, and people came out of the woodwork to help organize. They are great! Who would have thought?" I was pleased for him, but what is more important, I learned a lesson. There are always people who can lead. Just find them and give them a chance.

Did You Know

- Successful leaders use all their team's strengths. They recognize, develop, and use the physical, mental, and spiritual talents of their team members.
- Building a team requires great commitment.
- A sense of humor is vital to good leadership.

#24. Create a Creature

Ask the team to discuss and make a list of the characteristics of a good leader. After they list everything they can think of, they can use the attributes in their list to create a creature—the new leader. Label the parts on the creature and be sure all team members can explain why they have specific parts and what they mean in relation to leadership. For example, the leader may have oversized ears to convey the message that listening is an important part of leadership. Or the creature may be dressed in a coat of many colors because it must deal with many personalities. Discuss how this activity relates to helping select a team leader.

Materials You Will Need

construction paper

glue

tape

scissors

large chart paper

other materials one might use to make the creature

#25. Leader Reflection

Ask team members to think of the best leader they have ever worked for. Have them share their story with the group. When everyone has had a turn, ask them to list attributes these leaders had that made them favorites. Have the recorder write the attributes on a large piece of chart paper. Then ask them to clarify each of the attributes and reach consensus on the five they think are the most important. The team members can then decide who among them has these qualities.

Materials You Will Need

a piece of chart paper

a colored marker

masking tape

#26. Risk

Draw a chart with three columns labeled "Looks Like," "Sounds Like," and "Feels Like." Brainstorm with the team words that describe what a leader looks and sounds like. Then list words that describe the climate this leader would create in the "Feels Like" column. In the following meetings, give every team member a chance to be the leader for one team meeting. When everyone has had a chance to try out the role, lead a discussion about which person best fits the picture they created.

Materials You Will Need

a piece of chart paper labeled as directed

masking tape

a colored marker

Looks Like	Sounds Like	Feels Like

#27. Sold to the Highest Bidder

Ask the team to brainstorm 20 characteristics of a good leader. Have the recorder write the characteristics on a large piece of chart paper. Give each member $500 in play money. Distribute the money in different denominations. Ask for a volunteer to be the auctioneer. The auctioneer will auction off the different characteristics. Each team member buys the characteristics that he or she values most in a leader. Once everyone has spent his or her money, lead a discussion about why certain characteristics are valuable to them.

Materials You Will Need

$500 worth of play money for each team member

a piece of chart paper

a colored marker

masking tape

#28. I've Been There

Ask the team members to reflect on a time when they were in charge of something. It could be something in their personal lives such as the cake sale for a club, their child's Little League team, or planning a retirement party. The experience can be negative or positive. Ask them to tell the group what they learned about leadership from their experience. When everyone has had a turn, ask team members to tell which of the shared experiences stood out for them and why.

Materials You Will Need

THINGS THAT TAKE EFFORT: THE POWER OF ONE

No man will make a great leader who wants to do it all himself, or to get all the credit for doing it.

—Andrew Carnegie

Background

I received a call one day from a woman who wanted me to do a motivational keynote for the entire school system. When I asked her the topic, she replied that it was to be a special day for the school system in honor of all the hard work they had done that year. I talked to this woman a number of times nailing down details and so on. During one of our phone conversations I asked her what position she held in the school system. When she said, "superintendent," I almost fell out of my chair. She was the most unassuming leader I had ever met. When I arrived, she took me around to meet some of her people. The most memorable was when she passed the custodian, stopped, introduced me to him as if he were the superintendent, and then put her hand on his shoulder and asked him about his son, who was being shipped out to the Gulf War. I was so impressed with her respectful treatment of the staff. She seemed to be the kind of leader who gave all the credit to others and received a kingdom in return.

Did You Know

- When learning leadership skills, it is best to start out working on a single skill, to learn that skill well, and then begin developing the other skills one at a time.
- You cannot consistently behave in a way that is different from your self-image.
- Effective leaders help team members find their own ways of getting the job done better than before.
- Effective leaders know themselves.

#29. Big Book

Ask each team member to bring an article on leadership to the next meeting. As they share the articles, have them bring out important points. Ask the recorder to list the points on a chart. Then have the team synthesize all the articles by creating a Big Book. It is called a Big Book because the team creates a story about leadership with illustrations using chart paper and markers. Some examples I have seen are as follows:

Dorothy and the Wiz
The Adventures of Leaderperson
The Country Western Music Leadership Awards

The team writes its story around themes or ideas and interjects the main points on leadership from the articles.

When the team has finished its Big Book, lead a discussion about what they learned about leadership.

Materials You Will Need

several pieces of chart paper

assorted colored markers

glue

stapler and staples

scissors

construction paper

#30. Tell It Like It Is

Give each team member a handout with the following questions on it:

- What would appeal to you about being team leader?
- What would not appeal to you about being team leader?
- How do you think a leader influences a team?
- What would be stressful about being a leader?
- Why would the team want to follow you?
- What do you think are the most important qualities a leader must have?
- Who would make a good leader for our team?

Ask them to read the questions and reflect on them until the next team meeting when they will be asked to discuss their thoughts.

At the next team meeting, put each of the questions on a separate chart. There are seven questions, so there will be seven charts. Have each team member select a different colored magic marker. As members individually respond to the questions, they record answers on the charts using their colored marker.

At the end of the team meeting, ask them to think about everyone's responses for a week. During the next team meeting, have them discuss who on their team they want as the leader.

Materials You Will Need

7 pieces of chart paper

markers of assorted colors

masking tape

handout with questions

FOR THE COMMITTED: A GREAT VISIONARY

Leadership means vision, cheerleading, enthusiasm, love, trust, verve, passion, obsession, consistency, creating heroes, coaching, and numerous other things.

—Tom Peters

Background

I once knew a leader who had great vision. He had read all the books, had seen all the movies, and could quote all the quotes. He promised great things. In the day when everyone was crying the economic blues, he somehow found money to finance his vision. Sounds great, doesn't it? It could have been, but as he was telling his staff how much he knew and where he was going to lead them, he forgot to treat them with dignity. He started down the road to excellence, but no one followed. He wasn't worried, because he was the leader—he would push them. For three years he pushed,

and for three years they pushed back. He no longer pushes—
he was fired.

Did You Know

- Effective leaders allow and encourage regular learning and growth opportunities for the team.
- People don't care how much you know until they know how much you care.
- What team members really want is a leader whose competence and concern they can trust.
- It is the team leader who creates and maintains channels that enable the team to do its work.
- A leader cannot be imposed on a group. The leader must earn the right to lead even if he or she has been appointed.

#31. Empower or Bust

Give each team member a copy of *The Empowered Manager* by Peter Block (1987). Assign each team member a number of chapters to read. For example, if there are 10 chapters and five team members, assign each person 2 chapters to read. Give them two weeks to read and be ready to share with the entire team what they learn.

Once the team members discuss the entire book, they can discuss what they think "empowerment" means and how it relates to leadership. Together select a person to be the team leader who has the capacity to be an empowered leader.

Materials You Will Need

a copy of *The Empowered Manager* by Peter Block for each team member

#32. Who Will It Be?

After the team has met three or four times, distribute the Leadership Functions Check Sheet handout below to each team member. Ask team members to spend the next week completing the handout and bring it back to the next team meeting.

At the next meeting, make a large mockup of the handout and record each member's responses. Lead the team in a discussion of the responses and decide who seems to be emerging as the natural team leader. Ask that person if he or she would accept the role of team leader.

Materials You Will Need

1 Leadership Functions Check Sheet handout per team member

a colored marker

a big mockup of the Leadership Functions Check Sheet

Leadership Functions Check Sheet

Instructions: The following are kinds of leadership behavior that usually are engaged in by someone in a group. Read each item carefully and mark a check mark (✓) under the phrase that most accurately describes whoever performs that function in your team.

	No One	Formal Leader	Group Members (give names if possible)
1. Who usually brings together individual contributions?	———	———	———
2. Who ensures that the team makes decisions?	———	———	———
3. Who begins our meetings or starts our work?	———	———	———
4. Who keeps a check on whether objectives are set?	———	———	———
5. Who ensures that we follow an effective method of working together?	———	———	———
6. Who puts energy into the team to start us off or help us when we seem stuck?	———	———	———

7. Who watches over our operation and picks us up if we omit stages of working?	———	———
8. Who finds and brings in external information to help our work stay relevant?	———	———
9. Who represents us as a team with other groups or teams?	———	———
10. Who summarizes and clarifies after our discussions?	———	———
11. Who encourages contributions from team members?	———	———
12. Who supports other members in difficult situations?	———	———

Reprinted from Dave Francis and Don Young (1979). *Improving Work Groups: A Practical Manual for Team Building.* San Diego, CA: Pfeiffer & Company. Used with permission.

#33. Do Your Homework

Give each team member a copy of the handout I Think a Team Leader Should . . . Ask the members to complete it before the next team meeting. At the next meeting, ask each member to share his or her responses and compile a master list of each of the columns. Have the team members decide if they want a single leader or if they want to rotate leadership. Give the master list to the leader(s) to use as a guide.

I THINK A TEAM LEADER SHOULD . . .	
I think a leader should have the following abilities . . .	I would help the team reach its goals by . . .
I would build team cohesiveness by . . .	I would plan for the good of the group by . . .

Materials You Will Need

1 I Think A Team Leader Should . . . handout per person

1–2 pieces of chart paper

masking tape

a colored marker

#34. On Solid Ground

Have the team select a task or objective to complete within the hour. (Task suggestions: build a structure of straws at least four feet high, plan an overseas trip for the staff, design the government of the future.) Set up a video camera in the room to record what people say and do. Tell the group the camera is for giving them feedback later. Once they start working, they will forget the camera. When the task is complete, lead a team discussion about who they think emerged as the leader and why. They may have different opinions. Then play the video back and observe. Have them list all the leadership traits they see. Decide who emerged as the natural leader and see if that person would like to serve as the team's first leader.

Materials You Will Need

video camera

TV monitor

any materials for the task they are to complete

1 piece of chart paper

a colored marker

4

Establishing Roles and Responsibilities

I remember the first time I tried out for a play. The director handed me a script and said, "Read!" I had no idea what role I was reading. I looked up after a few minutes of reading only to see the director's lip curling into a disgusted sneer. With a wave of his hand he said, "No, no, no, nooo." He dismissed me, just like that. I was furious. I went to the back of the theater with the script and pouted for about 10 minutes. All of a sudden I was struck by the fact that I had failed not because I couldn't play the part, but because no one had clearly defined my role. I didn't know what I was responsible for. I opened the script, read the role, and began to visualize myself in the part. It took me about 30 minutes to get the role and responsibilities down. I lifted my head in the air and marched down the aisle to the director. I told him that I wanted to read for the part. He looked me up and down and said, "You've already had a chance. What makes you think you could do it now?" I looked him up and down and said, "Because I now have a clearly defined picture of the role I'm supposed to play." "Humph! Oh for heaven's sake, get on with it," he said. I did, and I won the role.

When I am in a training setting, I assign roles to all the participants at a table. They smile, laugh, accept the role, and then go through the training not really taking their role seriously. If team members do not take roles and responsibilities seriously, then they will end up doing what they have always done—that is, work as a committee. If a team is truly going to be effective, it must commit to doing things differently.

A team that wants to do things differently seriously considers what roles it needs for the team to function at its highest level. When the individual team members understand the roles, they can better understand the jobs of all the team members. They discover how they can work together to support each other in these roles. Establishing roles helps team members understand where they fit within the team and how they contribute to the achievement of the team's mission.

Teams also need to clarify role descriptions and select the right person for the role. *Role ambiguity* results when a team member does not have a clear picture of what is expected of him or her. *Role conflict* occurs when a person cannot perform an assigned role or has a picture of what constitutes the role that is different from that of his or her teammates.

It is important for team members to be successful in their roles. They can succeed if they use their special strengths and talents, evaluate their role, check their perceptions with other team members from time to time, and deal with problems and conflicts as they occur.

This chapter is designed to help teams clearly understand the type of roles needed and to understand the expectations of the roles. Working as a team to define roles and expectations will help inspire team members to achieve commitment and success and, what is more important, to accomplish their mission.

SIMPLE THINGS TO DO:
TURN THIS THING AROUND

Be yourself. Who else is better qualified?

—Anonymous

Background

In most of my workshops I ask participants to work in teams. The participants usually have fun with the process and do a lot of laughing and kidding. On this one day I told the small groups to select the person with the largest shoe size to be the team leader. As I watched them point and heard them laugh, I found myself smiling at my cleverness. All of a sudden a hand shot up from the back of the room. You know, the kind that goes up with such force it could launch a rocket—the kind you can't ignore. As I acknowledged the person, she rose out of her chair and said in a loud booming voice, "I don't appreciate being called Big Foot. I suggest in the future that you use something more appropriate. You have ruined my day. Not to mention I don't like my role." I was so stunned you could have knocked me over with a feather. I must admit that when I thought about it, I could see her point. I learned my lesson. I now give people a list of the roles and responsibilities and let them select the person that best fits the role.

Did You Know

- If the team is to be successful, everyone must be aware of the importance of roles.
- Everyone on the team must have a role.
- All roles are of equal importance.
- Everyone is accountable.
- When a team has problems, it's often because it hasn't clearly defined the roles.

#35. Everybody's in the Act

Distribute the Everybody's in the Act handout. Ask a team member to read the first set of directions in the first role box to select the Facilitator. Once this person has been selected, have the same team member move to the next box until all roles have been assigned. If there are more than five people on the team, the Timekeeper/Materials Specialist can be separated into two jobs. The team can decide on the duration of the roles. They may decide to change every few weeks, every month, and so on.

Materials You Will Need

1 Everybody's in the Act handout per team member

Everybody's in the Act

Once you have been selected for a part, you are not eligible for another role.

Casting directors are now filling the following roles. Please note how the positions will be filled.

Cast Responsibilities

Group interaction is key.
Roles are shared.
Members share responsibility for the group.
All members are equally important.

Count to 3. Point to a person. Whoever gets the most points becomes the **Facilitator.**

Role: *Keep group on task and make sure everyone has an equal opportunity to participate.*

Ask who has been in their field the longest. This person becomes the **Recorder.**

Role: *Record information team needs to have in order to process.*

Look around the group and select the person who is kind, upbeat, and likes people. This is the **Encourager.**

Role: *Give the team feedback on their team behaviors and cheer the team onward and upward.*

Select the person who likes to move around, wiggles a lot, and loves breaks. This is the **Timekeeper/Materials Specialist.**

Role: *Inform the team of time allotments and get all materials the team needs to perform activity.*

The remaining person becomes the **Spokesperson**.

Role: *Represent the team's thoughts to the total group.*

#36. Five-Card Draw

Put the roles and descriptions below on 4 × 6 cards. At the first team gathering, ask each person to draw a card and read the role and role description. The members then discuss which roles would best suit them. Feel free to add to role descriptions.

Card 1—Leader	Card 2—Recorder
• keep team on task • make sure everyone participates • lead the discussion for the next agenda	• record the minutes • do chart work if necessary
Card 3—Timekeeper	**Card 4—Materials Person**
• keep up with time and give 10-minute warning, 5-minute warning, etc., so meeting doesn't run over allotted time	• bring necessary materials to the meeting • set up meeting space if any equipment is needed
Card 5—Observer	**Card 6—Encourager**
• collect data on teaming skills and give feedback on how the team is doing	• tell the team when they do something well and encourage them when they are down
Card 7—Question Captain	**Card 8—Checker**
• make sure all questions are answered or will be answered by next meeting • keep a list of important questions	• check the team's perceptions of what is going on

Materials You Will Need

1 set of role cards

#37. You're Up

Bring the set of role cards listed in Activity #36 (Five-Card Draw) to the team meeting. Ask each person to select a card and play that role for one team meeting. At the end of the team meeting, redistribute the role cards so that everyone will have a different role for the next meeting. When everyone has had an opportunity to do all the roles, have a team meeting and decide who best fits what role. If they agree to accept, they keep that role for the year or whatever time the team designates.

Materials You Will Need

   1 set of role cards from Activity #36

#38. Watch Where You Sit

At a team meeting, place a set of role cards (from Activity #36) face down in the chairs where the team members will sit. Each person is responsible for the role that is in his or her chair for that day. Team members can always swap roles.

Materials You Will Need

   1 set of role cards from Activity #36

#39. Sign on the Dotted Line

During a team meeting, lead the team in a brainstorming session about all the possible roles the team needs to function. As team members come up with role descriptions, have one team member write the roles and descriptions on a laminated chart. Whoever gets to the next team meeting first signs up for the role he or she would like to have for the meeting. The next person who arrives signs up for the role of his or her choice, and so on. The members may trade or try to bargain for the role of their choice, but they may not harass or make a team member feel bad if he or she doesn't want to trade.

Leader	_Megan_
Recorder	_Nancy_
Timekeeper	_Peter_
Encourager	_Rhonda_

Materials You Will Need

a laminated chart

a colored marker

#40. Slap a Role

Have the team gather around a table while one person slowly turns the role cards (from Activity #36) over. When team members see the roles they want for the day, the first member to slap the card gets that role. If no one slaps some of the role cards, just put them back in the deck and keep using them until everyone has a role.

Materials You Will Need

1 set of role cards from Activity #36

THINGS THAT TAKE EFFORT: HIGH HOPES

I feel the greatest reward is the opportunity to do more.

— Jonas Salk

Background

Are you ever amazed that anything in this world gets done? I am! I work with thousands of smart, well-meaning people each year, and yet when I observe teams working together, I notice some interesting behaviors. For example, have you ever noticed in some team meetings that everyone is leading? Or even more interesting, no one is leading? I have heard team members say, "No, you do it!" Another one says, "Not me, you do it!" This goes back and forth until finally a member says, "Oh heck, I'll do it! But you're going to do it next time."

I think one of the funniest things I've heard while observing a team was the following exchange among three members.

"Did you bring the stuff?"

"What stuff?"

"Whatever someone was supposed to bring to the meeting."

"I didn't bring it. Maybe Rose brought it."

"I don't know what you're talking about."

"Oh well, no big deal. It must not have been important since we can't remember what it was or who was supposed to bring it. Maybe someone else knows."

I finally figured out that the reason these things happen has nothing to do with intelligence. It has to do with never having sat down as a team and discussed roles and responsibilities. I have learned that even a simple approach to roles and role descriptions is better than nothing. I have also learned that the more effort a team puts into this, the more successful the team will be.

Did You Know

- A role is a person's place on the team—the part he or she expects to play and that others expect that person to play.
- Defining roles and responsibilities is one of the most challenging problems a team faces.
- Once teams learn about roles and responsibilities and realize the importance of them, it is fairly easy to correct problems.
- You seldom have to coerce, goad, or force team members to work in a team when they have clearly defined roles.

#41. My Momma Told Me Not to Brag But . . .

This activity is designed to give the team members an opportunity to reflect on the roles that are available and that they feel they could do well. Put the following list of roles and descriptions on a chart, blackboard, or overhead:

Roles

Team Facilitator leads discussion, keeps people on task, helps enforce behavior norms

Leader represents the team at other meetings, takes issues to the administration, supports the team and takes care of distributing minutes to administrator, steps in to resolve conflict if facilitator needs help

Scribe keeps the minutes for the team meetings, reads any parts to the team that they call for, keeps a team copy and gets one ready for the leader to give to the supervisor

Observer collects informal data concerning teaming skills and role performance in order to give the team feedback on how they are doing

Encourager keeps the team's spirits up, helps design ways the team can celebrate their successes and learn from mistakes

Timekeeper keeps the team aware of the time frame they have agreed to work in, gives time updates such as "10 minutes to go," and so on

Materials Person makes sure the team has the resources they need for the meeting

Tell the team they have 10 minutes to read and think about the different roles. Then go around the table and ask each person to say what role he or she would do well and why. The team decides who will have what role and for how long.

Materials You Will Need

a list of the roles and role descriptions on a chart, blackboard, or overhead

#42. Put It in the Job Description

Write the roles from Activity #41 on a chart, blackboard, or overhead but leave the descriptions out. Have a discussion about how the team thinks the roles should be described. Write the role descriptions based on their conversation. These become the team roles. The team can use any of the activities in this chapter to assign the roles.

Materials You Will Need

1 role list from Activity #41

#43. Take a Letter

Ask team members to write a letter to the team describing the role they want. They must list 5 to 10 reasons why they should have the role and list three things they will do to be sure they do a good job. The team members listen to everyone, then decide who gets what role.

Materials You Will Need

a piece of paper and a pencil for each team member

#44. A Team Effort

Using the role list from Activity #41, write the roles on a chart, blackboard, or overhead without the descriptions. The team may want to look at the roles listed and add or delete some. Give everyone a large sheet of paper and ask them to make a web for each role (see the illustration for a web model from Activity 17). For example, if there are nine roles, there will be nine webs, and so on. Have them spend a few minutes on each role webbing words that describe what the role should entail. Next, have a large web for each role on a chart at the front of the meeting room. Start with a role and ask team members for words that best describe the role. When each role has been webbed with contributions from the entire team, write a role description for each one.

Materials You Will Need

a large piece of paper and a colored marker per team member

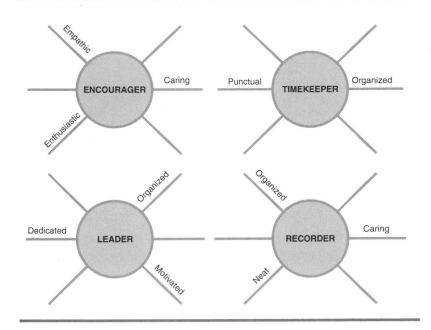

1 piece of chart paper per role from Activity #41

masking tape

#45. Door Number One, Two, or Three?

List the roles and descriptions from Activity #41 on a chart, blackboard, or overhead. Ask the team to discuss the roles and decide if any should be added or deleted. Give team members a piece of paper and ask them to list their first, second, and third preferences for a role. Have team members look at the lists and use them to distribute roles. Make an effort to give people a role they prefer.

Materials You Will Need

role list and descriptions from Activity #41 on a chart, blackboard, or overhead

a piece of paper and a pencil for each team member

For the Committed:
If They Could See Me Now!

Use what talents you possess. The woods would be very silent if no birds sang there except those that sang best.

—Anonymous

Background

I remember a conversation I once had with Dr. Rosemary Lambie, my mentor and friend. We were talking about using people. She told me that when it came to getting people to do a job, if I used them well I would always be successful. At first I wasn't quite sure what she meant, but as I grew older and more experienced, I realized that when people are doing a job they like and can do successfully, you never have to ask them twice or worry about whether it will get done. I believe this holds true for teaming. If the team members take the time to think of the roles they need to have, and give them to the appropriate people, the performance level of the team will skyrocket.

Did You Know

- Well done is better than well said.
- Once the team defines and accepts its roles, it experiences a dramatic increase in cohesiveness.
- Team members must not only be responsible for their individual roles but also must support the roles of others.
- Feedback on performance is necessary to be successful in a role.
- When a team works together to define roles, it helps to inspire each member's commitment.

#46. Storming

Lead the team in a review of its mission statement. As people review their mission, ask them to brainstorm all the possible roles they need in order to have a quality team. Once they get a list, they can write their role descriptions. They then match roles to the team members who are best qualified. They may take two or three meetings to decide who would be best for the roles. Some team members may want to try the role for a few weeks, receive feedback from the team members, and then decide if it's the best role for them. During this time, suggest that the team members interview other successful teams and compare roles. They may want to add new roles they hadn't thought of or change the descriptions as they become more familiar with teaming. The key is to monitor constantly and adjust the roles to make them more efficient.

Materials You Will Need

a copy of the team's mission statement

a large piece of paper

a colored marker

#47. Go Fishing

Before the next team meeting, give each member six large index cards and ask them to write on each card a characteristic of themselves that they bring to the team. Ask them to write three positive characteristics and three characteristics that may not be positive. For example, a positive characteristic might be "having a sense of humor." A negative one might be "stickler about time." Have everyone share their cards and hang them on the wall. Then have them brainstorm all the roles the team needs in order to function at a quality level. Place a list of the roles on the wall. Next have them write the descriptions of the roles. Once this is done, have them look at the characteristics on the wall and determine who would be best for a specific role. For example, the person who is a stickler for time would be a great timekeeper. This person would help the team abide by the time limits and at the same time would be happy because he or she would be sure that things started and ended on time.

Materials You Will Need

> 6 large index cards per team member
>
> masking tape
>
> 1 piece of chart paper
>
> a colored marker

#48. You Get What You Expect

Have the team members use one of the activities in this chapter to establish what roles they need for their team to function. After each team member has had a role for a month, give out the What Did I Expect? worksheet. Ask each member to complete it and bring it to the next team meeting.

At the next team meeting, ask each team member to share what he or she has written on the handout, column by column. After reading each column, have the team member ask for comments from the group. When everyone has had a turn, ask the team members to share how this activity will help them be more successful in their role. Make a list of how they will support each other, using their comments.

What Did I Expect?		
What I expected from my role	*What I am discovering about my role*	*Support I need to do my role*

Materials You Will Need

1 What Did I Expect? handout per person

a large piece of chart paper

a colored marker

masking tape

#49. That's What I Like!

You can't do this activity until the team members have their roles and have done them for a while. Every few months or so, put a chart on the wall with the headings "What I like best about my role," "What I like least about my role," and "I could do my role better if . . ." Ask each member to respond while the recorder writes the responses in the appropriate column. The team discusses the responses as they see fit.

Now ask each team member to select a partner. Have each pair get a piece of chart paper and two markers (one color for each person). Ask them to divide the chart paper into three columns and label it as follows:

Ask each person to give the other person feedback. For example, under the first column, one might say and write, "What you do well as a leader is to make sure that we all treat each other with dignity. You check to see that we still understand the mission."

What you do well as a ___	What can I do to help you in your role as ___	An idea I had about your role is ___

Materials You Will Need

> 3 charts for the first three questions
>
> masking tape
>
> 1 piece of chart paper per pair
>
> 2 different color markers per pair

#50. Grumble, Grit, and Groan!

This activity is a good one to do after the team members have had a role assignment for a month or so. Ask the team to stand up and begin talking simultaneously about their roles. They can complain and share reservations, resentments, gripes, or concerns. When they run out of things to grumble about, have them let out a loud groan and sit down. When you think the team has had enough time to get some of the negative energy out, call time. Then have the team focus on the following questions:

How did you feel during this exercise?

What are the benefits of this exercise?

What issues do we need to discuss?

Are we ready to move on?

Materials to Be Used

> a set of questions on a chart, blackboard, or overhead

5

Code of Conduct

A large school district hired me to head up its staff development department. I had no sooner arrived at the central office and sat down at my desk than I heard a knock on my door. I looked up to see two of my soon-to-be best friends standing at my door. I smiled, greeted them warmly, and was just about to say something funny when I noticed they had very serious looks on their faces. I immediately wiped the smile from my face and said, "What's up?" Their eyes shifted from side to side, scoping out the area. They lowered their voices, entered the office, closed the door, and said, "We have some things we need to tell you about working here." I found myself whispering in reply, "Tell me, is it dangerous?" "No, no," they replied, "but there are some unwritten rules around here. If you happen to break one, you will be in BIG trouble." They filled me in for the next 30 minutes. I took notes and was happily employed there for six years.

Organizations, groups, committees, and teams will automatically develop a code of conduct. The most effective of these will be ones in which input from the employees has been solicited and agreed upon.

I define a team as a group of five to nine people who are highly energetic, work well together, respect each other, work toward common goals, and produce high-quality results. Clearly, having people skills is essential to team success.

This chapter is about team members taking responsibility for and establishing their own norms and standards. It is about holding each other accountable for excellence. Most teams do not do this step in the teaming process. They use a reactive approach rather than a proactive approach. They wait until something goes wrong to set norms for the team.

This chapter is important because it establishes the culture of the team. When I say "culture," I mean "the way we do things around here." The culture a team wants to develop is one of inclusiveness, a feeling that everyone on the team is welcome. There is no pressure to conform. Different styles are accepted. The team members are committed to one another.

Another characteristic that the culture should strive for is realism. Teams need to look at a problem and come up with the most realistic solution, a solution not based on politics, favoritism, or any other superfluous reason. Somewhere in the code of conduct, norms need to be established so that people have permission to be heard. In this climate, if the team is going astray, someone will speak up and say, "Wait a minute, I can't go along with this." An important part of realism is humility. Team members appreciate the gifts other team members have and begin to recognize their own limitations. This helps build interdependence on the team. Think about it—would you rather work with an arrogant team or a humble one?

A team needs to build a culture of contemplation. This means the team has discussed and established a number of ways to examine itself. Teams must begin self-examination right from the start. No team will automatically stay in good health. When the team needs to recover from something, they focus on recovery. They will drop the current task or goal and heal themselves. This is one more major difference between a committee and a team. A committee continues on at all costs to get the task done. On a team, the task and maintenance of the team are equally important.

The team culture should be one that makes the team meeting a safe place. A safe place is created through trust and team norms that foster safety. Active listening, ways to handle conflict, and, most important, how to treat each other with dignity should all be part of team norms. The team will need to discuss what dignity looks like, sounds like, and feels like.

A team needs a culture that can fight with dignity. There will be issues that come up that make team members examine their values. Sometimes an issue may call for rethinking some of those values, a very emotional prospect. In many instances, conflict is healthy, but teams must establish norms for conflict or it can get out of hand.

A team needs to develop a spirit. The team should delight in itself and the work it does. I am not talking about a competitive spirit in which one work team thinks it is better than another work team. A true sense of spirit is one of peace. It is one where there is a strong bond of caring, a real sense of wisdom, consensual decision making, and respectful treatment of others.

SIMPLE THINGS TO DO: I JUST DROPPED IN TO SEE WHAT CONDITION MY CONDITION WAS IN

When you care, you win. Too many people are so involved in getting the job done or in doing what they consider their own work they forget to use common sense—which is treating other people as you know you would like to be treated.

—Donna Edton, Vice President, Campbell Soup Company

Background

I have been doing team training a number of years now, and never once when I ask people to tell me what they know do they ever mention setting norms for team behavior. It's as if they think it will just happen. When we get to the section on developing the team's code of conduct, you would think I had given them the keys to the kingdom. They say if they had not learned anything else but code of conduct, the time would have been well spent. They thank me and tell me how wise I am. Somehow I just can't bring myself to tell them I didn't discover code of conduct—someone taught me.

Did You Know

- Teams will automatically develop a code of conduct or standard operating procedure; the question is, is it effective?
- Every team should develop norms of behavior for the team to follow.
- Teams, like individuals, have short attention spans.
- Ignoring the mechanics of teamwork will undoubtedly lead to trouble.

#51. Play by the Rules

Ask the group to brainstorm a list of rules that will help the team function smoothly. Write the rules on a piece of chart paper. Once the team completes the brainstorm, have everyone look at the list and clarify any rules that are not clear. Then ask the group to see if some of the suggestions are the same. If so, eliminate duplicates. Next ask the team to look at the list and categorize the ideas. For example, there may be ideas on the list that have to do with how members treat each other during a discussion. That category would be called Discussion Norms. All the items that have to do with discussion go under that category. Have the team go through the entire list. Once all the categories have been made, have the team take each one and develop norms and rules. If there are seven categories, there will be seven norms, and so forth. The team now has a set of norms by which it will operate. From time to time, you may need to revise or add to them.

Materials You Will Need

1 piece of chart paper for the brainstorm

8–10 pieces of chart paper to use for the different categories

masking tape

a colored marker

#52. Survival on Mars

Distribute a copy of the Survival on Mars handout to each team member. Tell them to read the directions very carefully, starting with Step 1. Remind them that Steps 2 and 3 are to be done alone, and Step 4 is a team effort. Ask one person to be the observer. Tell the observer that he or she is to watch the team intently and record all behaviors. For example, the observer might record that all the team members talked at once, or that one person made fun of someone's idea, or that one person didn't participate. At the end of 30 minutes, stop the team. Next the observer shares the list of observed behaviors. The team listens and then decides what kind of team rules they might need in order to work together successfully. They draft a list of norms. Once the list is drafted, they have a team discussion for clarification. The norms they develop become the rules for the way the team members treat each other.

Materials You Will Need

1 Survival on Mars handout per team member

a large piece of chart paper and a colored marker

a piece of paper and a pencil for each team member

masking tape

SURVIVAL ON MARS

You and your teammates have landed on Mars. The planet is inhabited by unfriendly aliens who have told you they will spare your life only if you and your team can create a successful school for their 40 children of all ages. They are going to give you two days to come up with one. The curriculum is up to you. You can send only one supply list back to Earth requesting 10 items. What 10 items would you choose to have sent?

Step 1 Decide with the team if you are going to stay on Mars and try to establish a school or if you are going to try to escape.

Step 2 Each team member makes a list of the 10 items to be sent by rocket from Earth.

Step 3 Each team member rank orders his or her items from first choice to last choice, with Number 1 being the first choice, and so on.

Step 4 The team members share their items and reach consensus on the top 10 items they will have sent from Earth.

Note: If yours is not a school team, change the word *school* to whatever organization you are working with. For example, if your team works for a hospital, have it establish a hospital that would help the aliens become healthier. This is a versatile activity. The idea is to have an activity in which people can be observed while working together.

#53. How Can I Help?

Lead the team in a group discussion of behaviors that will help the team function effectively. Have the team recorder make a list of the suggestions on a large piece of chart paper. Ask if they need any clarification. Ask the recorder to put the following statements on a chart:

I'm good at _____ , so when _____ happens, I'll be responsible for _____.

As the team members look at the behaviors listed on the chart, they choose one they think they could do and make a statement such as, "I'm good at staying on task, so when the team has been off task over five minutes, I'll be responsible for getting them back on task by giving a signal." Have the recorder record the responses on the chart. Each team member should be responsible for something on the list. Some team members may take more than one. After the team has accounted for the entire list, it can use this chart as the norms for behavior during the team meetings.

Materials You Will Need

several pieces of chart paper

masking tape

a colored marker

#54. Problems? What Problems?

Tell the team members they are going to have an opportunity to reflect on all the possible problems that could occur that would keep the team from functioning at its highest level. As they think of all the possible problems that could occur, they write each problem on a 4 × 6 card and put it in a box. Once all the cards are in, let each person pull one out, read the problem, and offer a suggestion about how to handle it. The team may add suggestions. After the team members have discussed all problems, ask them to talk about how this activity relates to them and how they could use it to make them a stronger team.

Materials You Will Need

3–4 4 × 6 index cards per team member

pencils or colored markers

#55. Metaphors or Bust

Put each of the following metaphors on a separate piece of chart paper and ask the team to complete the sentences. The recorder records the responses.

A team that has norms is an ocean because . . .

A team that works well together is a present because . . .

A team that works well together is a superhighway because . . .

Read the metaphors and lead the team in a discussion about why they need to develop a set of norms right away, as opposed to waiting until they have met a few times. Then ask each team member to take a week to think of some norms that are important for the team to have. They are to come to the next meeting with their suggestions. At that time, the team will decide which norms they will use for their team.

Materials You Will Need

several pieces of chart paper

colored markers

masking tape

#56. Let's Be Sensible

Put the Multisensory Chart on an easel or give a copy of the chart to the team.

Tell the team members to think about the idea of norms and rules. Ask them to come up with five words in each category that describe what rules would feel like, look like, smell like, taste like, and sound like.

Multisensory Chart

When the team has completed the chart, they are to make a metaphor using at least one word from each box. They may add words. Once they complete the metaphor, lead the team in a discussion about why norms and rules are essential in order to function.

Multisensory Chart

Looks Like

    a box
    a harbor
    a line

Feels Like

    warm fuzzies
    velvet
    cozy fire

Smells Like

    perfume
    coffee brewing
    campfire

Tastes Like

    honey
    bittersweet chocolate
    salsa

Sounds Like

    a cheering crowd
    a symphony
    a cat purring

Materials You Will Need

    1 copy of the Multisensory Chart

    1 piece of chart paper

    colored markers

    masking tape

#57. Why Should We?

Explain to the team that they are going to be discussing team norms and rules from three different angles. Place a blank PCI Chart on the blackboard or on a large sheet of chart paper.

Explain that the *P* stands for *positive,* the *C* stands for *concerns,* and the *I* stands for *interesting.* Lead the team in a discussion about some positive points of having team rules, some concerns about having team rules, and interesting things about having team rules. Have the recorder record the responses on the chart under the appropriate letters. Invite the team members to set a time to select a procedure from this book that will enable them to develop a set of norms and rules for their team.

P	C	I
will add structure to our meetings	rules may be hard to enforce	we've never tried rules before
we might get more done	rules might feel artificial	if it works for debates, it might work for us

Materials You Will Need

1 PCI chart

a colored marker

masking tape

THINGS THAT TAKE EFFORT: PUTTING IT TOGETHER

Did you ever see a committee of five work? One man does all the work; two men tell him how to do it; one man pats him on the back for doing it well; and the fifth man keeps the minutes of the meeting.

—Anonymous

Background

Not long ago a school asked me to visit and observe its teams in action. My role was to observe their team members' behaviors, ask them if they needed any additional help, and find out how things were going. I visited a number of teams that day, and I saw a variety of behaviors, but I'll never forget one team—the one the principal said was the best. When I arrived, they were sitting randomly throughout the classroom. One was grading papers, and one kept telling everyone to hurry up. There was no agenda. Someone just started talking. Some members were listening and some were not. Somehow they got on the topic of how they made decisions. The leader said he just did what he thought was best whenever he couldn't get everyone together. Someone said, "You do?!" It was dropped. They spent some time complaining about how things were working. They didn't decide on, or even discuss, solutions. At the end of the hour, nothing had happened. The strange part of it was that they told me they really enjoyed teaming and wouldn't want to go back to the old way of doing business. You know what? I believe them. They were doing the best they knew how to do. This team had never heard of a code of conduct.

Did You Know

- Team guidelines usually prevent misunderstandings and disagreements.
- An effective and productive team does not develop by accident.
- The more individuals share in and agree on group norms, the more likely they will be to like each other.
- How the team works together determines how effective it will be.
- The team should be open and flexible to new ways of doing things.

#58. Absolutely Necessary

Lead the team in a discussion about what rules are absolutely necessary in order for the team to work productively. If a team member has a problem with any of the rules, put the Group Behavior Problem Chart on the blackboard or a piece of chart paper and have the team go through it. For example, a team member might say, "I have a problem with the rule that has been suggested that we only have only one minute per person when discussing something. I can't go with that." You would then take the team through the analysis so that the person with the concern has an opportunity to share his or her feelings. You also want to be sure that the team doesn't just throw out what may be a good norm. All that may be needed are minor adjustments to the rule or norm.

Group Behavior Problem Chart

1. Review information about the problem.
2. Define the behavior the team would like to have.
3. Brainstorm the options.
4. Agree and act on the team's choices.

Materials You Will Need

1 Group Behavior Problem Chart

a colored marker

masking tape

#59. I Hate It When . . .

Ask each team member to think of a time they worked with a group of people and got upset because of a specific behavior. Tell them to list on a piece of paper at least five behaviors that irritate them in groups. Each person shares. The recorder records the responses. Help the team to reach consensus on the top five irritating behaviors. Team members discuss the five and spend time developing norms so that these behaviors do not occur on their team.

Materials You Will Need

1 piece of chart paper

a colored marker

masking tape

a piece of paper and a pencil for each team member

#60. What's Happening?

After the team has met four or five times, give each team member the What's Happening? handout. Ask them to complete it and be ready to share it at the next team meeting. At the next team meeting, ask the members to share their responses. The recorder records the responses. After everyone shares, invite the team to discuss what they need to do to carry out some of the suggestions.

What's Happening?

1. What three behaviors helped the team function smoothly?

2. One thing I could have done to help the team work together is . . .

3. One thing I think the other team members could do to help the team work together is . . .

Materials You Will Need

1 What's Happening? handout per person (see above)

1 piece of chart paper

a colored marker

masking tape

#61. What's the Word?

Lead the team in a discussion about all the norms they think are necessary for the team to function. As team members come up with norms, have the recorder write them on a piece of chart paper for all to see. Once you have a list of norms you all are satisfied with, turn the team's attention to the Norms Analysis Chart. Ask the recorder to put the first norm in the column marked "Norm." Decide together if that norm is one the team needs to work on, or if it is no problem. Put a check mark in the appropriate column and then write a comment. Do this for all the norms on your list. When you are finished, return to the norms you need to work on and devise an action plan for working on them.

NORM	NEED TO WORK ON	NO PROBLEM	COMMENTS
1. Take turns speaking	✓		We interrupt each other sometimes, especially when we disagree.
2. End meetings on time		✓	We're good at timekeeping.
3. Everyone does his or her fair share	✓		Some people end up doing more than others because some people are busier to begin with.

Materials You Will Need

> 1 piece of chart paper
>
> a colored marker
>
> 1 Norms Analysis Chart

#62. Turning Wrongs Into Rights

Lead the team members in a discussion of behaviors they do not like to see when working in a group. Keep listing the responses on a piece of chart paper until you have about 10 responses. Lead them in a second discussion about behaviors they like to see when working in a group. They must tell why they like these specific behaviors. Record about 10 or so of these behaviors on a second chart. On a third piece of chart paper, they are to transform each behavior on the first list into a behavior they would like. Have the team destroy the first list with flair (shred it up, stomp on it, or whatever). Next have the team focus on the third list now and discuss how they can incorporate those behaviors into their team's functioning.

Materials You Will Need

> 3 pieces of chart paper
>
> colored markers
>
> masking tape

FOR THE COMMITTED: ONLY THE STRONG SURVIVE

The hardest thing to give is in.

—Anonymous

Background

I often use the story of General Pickett and General Grant when I talk about people working together for the good of the team. Rumor has it that one evening after a battle, General Grant's men were camped on one side of a river and General Pickett's on the other. General Pickett had lost. That evening

General Grant heard all kinds of singing and shouting from the other side of the river. He was perplexed. Why would defeated soldiers be celebrating? He sent his scouts to see what was going on. They returned with the news that General Pickett's wife had just given birth to a son. General Grant told his men to light fires all down the river and to shout congratulations. Even in times of great strife, there are rules that men live by out of respect for each other.

Did You Know

- Teams with a code of conduct are more cohesive. The meetings are often noisy, full of personal byplay, disagreement, and even conflict, but it's done within limits.
- It's important for teams to work reflectively, creatively, and productively.
- All teams have a rhythm that alternates between relaxed and freewheeling discussion and well-ordered procedures.
- Groups strongly influence the behavior of their members by setting and enforcing norms.
- Individual team member acceptance is often based on how that team member conforms to the team's norms.

#63. Let's Do It Right

In a team discussion, ask the team if they agree not to go any further until they have established team norms. If so, discuss whether and how to go about researching similar organizations that have already established teams that are successful. The team could ask for time to visit and ask the teams what has made them successful. When they return to their organization, they can begin to establish their norms. Make sure they have established norms for the following:

Team Meetings: time, place, room arrangement

Team Participation: procedure to make sure everyone is heard

Problem Solving: a method they will use when they have a problem

Resources: how they go about getting what they need

Conflict: how they will deal with conflict

Decisions: how they will decide what technique to use for decision making

Complaints: productive procedure for handling complaints

Team Discussion: how they will handle summarizing, moving on, and so on

Evaluation: how they will evaluate the team's progress

Celebrations: how the team will celebrate

Training: how to decide what additional training they will need

The team may choose some specific team training it will need in order to learn about problem solving and conflict management. This procedure for norm development may take one or two months. This list is not exhaustive, but it is a good beginning for the committed.

Materials You Will Need

The materials will depend on what the team decides to do. For example, if they decide to get additional training, they will need to ask the person conducting the training what materials they will need.

6

Managing Meetings

Shakespeare, in his play As You Like It, says, "All the world's a stage, and all the men and women merely players." If I could rewrite this line for a modern-day saga, it would go, "All the world's a business meeting, and all the men and women merely passive, bored, frustrated players." Take today. I decided to take an hour break from the writing of this book. "Why not make some phone calls?" I said. I made 10 calls. Only one person was in. Where were the rest of the people? You got it—in meetings. In fact, some of the people were going to be in meetings ALL day.

Team members need to view their meetings as important gatherings. If people consider meetings a waste of time, then eventually apathy will set in, team members will drag in late, and attendance will drop. One of the ways to keep meetings important is to have them only when they are necessary. I once visited a team whose members were upset because their schedule included an hour and 30 minutes a day to meet. I asked them if they had brainstormed other alternatives. They looked at me with shock written all over their faces. "We can do that?" they said.

Remember, when to meet and how long to meet are the team's decisions. The team I described above decided to have an hour team meeting daily and 30 minutes for individual tasks.

They went away feeling happy and looking forward to their new schedule.

Are there guidelines about when to meet and when not to meet? Michael Doyle and David Straus (1976), in their book *How to Make Meetings Work*, give the following guidelines:

WHEN TO HAVE A MEETING

Specifically, if you are a manager or a chairperson, calling a meeting may be a good idea when

> you want information or advice from your group

> you want to involve your group in solving a problem or making a decision

> there is an issue that needs to be clarified

> you have concerns you want to share with your group as a whole

> the group itself wants a meeting

> there is a problem that involves people from different groups, or

> there is a problem and it's not clear what it is or who is responsible for dealing with it

WHEN NOT TO HAVE A MEETING

A meeting is generally not a good idea when

> you have to deal with personnel issues like hiring, firing, and negotiating salaries

> there is inadequate data or poor preparation

> something could be communicated better by telephone, memo, or a one-on-one discussion

the subject matter is so confidential or secret that it can't be shared with some group members

your mind is made up and you have already made your decision

the subject is trivial, or

there is too much anger and hostility in the group, and people need time to calm down before they begin to work collaboratively.

We are a meeting society. That is why this chapter is important. It will give your team practical techniques for improving the quality of your meetings. People will come away from the team meetings feeling productive, happy, and successful. Productivity will go up. Time, our most precious resource, will not be wasted. Most important, the team will work constructively and productively toward its mission.

SIMPLE THINGS TO DO: WHAT KIND OF FOOL AM I?

Few people know how to hold a meeting. Even fewer know how to let it go.

—Robert Fuoss

Background

I can still remember the excitement of my first year on the staff of a large southern university. I reported to work the first day full of vim, vigor, and enthusiasm. As I entered the outer office, my heart skipped a beat as I spied my very own mail slot—CAROL SCEARCE. As I reached into the box I pulled out my first piece of correspondence: ATTENTION . . . ALL FACULTY . . . MEETING 9:00 A.M. TODAY. I remember thinking

I was glad I had come in early. Gosh, what would have happened if I hadn't checked my mail? I would have missed the meeting! As the clock struck 8:30 a.m., I pulled out my meeting announcement to see where the meeting was to be held. "Ummm, it must be here somewhere. Oh well, I'd better ask." I didn't want to mess up my first day. As I wandered down the hall asking my colleagues where the meeting was, they all responded in a very bored tone, "Who knows?" I was wild; it was almost 9:00. I was going to be late. I began frantically looking in every room. As I opened the sixth door, I heard someone behind me. It was my department chairperson. My eyes lit up; I was saved. He smiled at me and said, "Hi, where's the meeting?"

The next year as I entered the outer office I automatically pulled the announcement for the first meeting out of my mailbox. As I stood there reading, the new kid on the block walked up to me full of vim, vigor, and enthusiasm and said, "Hi, I'm Pat! Can you tell me where we will be meeting?" I rolled my eyes and with a bored expression responded, "Who knows?"

Did You Know

- The results of a meeting affect the functioning of the team and its ability to achieve its objectives.
- Unnecessary meetings are time wasters; meetings should be used only when truly necessary.
- The average person will sit through more than 9,000 hours of meetings in his or her lifetime.
- Team meetings directly affect how individuals feel about their team, how committed they are to decisions, and how well they work as a team and individually.
- Many people view meetings as a necessary evil.

#64. Picture This

Ask the team members to think of the best meeting they have ever attended. Give them about 10 minutes to individually brainstorm and write down the reasons that meeting was successful. Pass out blank index cards. Ask them to create a visual representation or snapshot of the reasons on the index cards. If a team member has five reasons on his or her brainstorm list, then there will be five snapshots. Have each team member explain his or her snapshots. Then glue each snapshot to a large piece of paper that represents a photo album of what a successful meeting should look like. Use this photo album, along with an activity in this book, to develop procedures for successful meetings.

Materials You Will Need

a piece of paper and a pencil for each team member

4–5 index cards for each team member

a large piece of chart paper or chart paper cut into the size of a photo album

glue

assorted colored markers

masking tape

#65. Stand and Be Counted

Place the following statement on a chart or blackboard:

Eyes roll, tongues wag, people sigh, a feeling of dread fills the place when a meeting of any sort is announced.

Ask the team members to discuss what the statement means, why it is or isn't an accurate portrayal of meetings, and any other thoughts they may have. Next, place the following statements on a chart or a blackboard and ask everyone to respond. The recorder records the comments.

So, why have meetings? Could we do without them? Why or why not?

Spend 10 or 15 minutes responding to the two questions. Then tell the team members that it is a fact that as we move through the twenty-first century, the vast majority of organizations couldn't function without meetings. In light of this fact, how can we be sure that our team meetings are well organized and productive? As the team discusses this, the recorder records the responses on a chart.

Materials You Will Need

chart or blackboard with the quote

chart or blackboard with the questions from the activity

a colored marker

masking tape

#66. It's Been My Observation That . . .

Tell the team members that since they haven't received much training in how to hold team meetings, they are going to learn from each meeting. Ask each team member to keep a team journal in which they record their thoughts and ideas about how the team meetings go and what they can do to improve them. Have the members collect this data for at least five team meetings. Devote the sixth team meeting to a team sharing of their data collection. The recorder records the ideas on a chart for future use. The team then decides the next steps it needs to take.

Materials You Will Need

a notebook to be used as a journal per team member

a piece of chart paper

a colored marker

masking tape

#67. Where I Come From We . . .

Tell the team members that they are going to dialogue about team meetings. Explain that a dialogue and a discussion are two different things. In a dialogue, there is free and creative exploration of complex and subtle issues, a deep listening to one another, and a suspension of one's own views. In a discussion, different views are presented and defended and one view is selected.

The team members are to dialogue about what they think of meetings. What makes a meeting exciting, productive, and challenging? What makes a meeting unsuccessful?

Have the team sit in a circle with no barriers (such as a table) between members. Each team member dialogues about his or her thoughts with no interruptions, judgments, or other kinds of distracting behaviors. Each team member has an opportunity to express himself or herself. The entire team actively listens. After the dialogue, put the following T-Chart on the blackboard or chart paper.

Lead the team in a discussion of the two questions while the recorder records the main points members make. After the discussion, the members choose the next steps they need to take to ensure that their meetings are effective.

T-CHART

What we know	What we need to do

Materials You Will Need

a copy of the T-Chart

a colored marker

masking tape

THINGS THAT TAKE EFFORT: THE GREAT PRETENDER

Individual commitment to a group effort—that is what makes a team work, a company work, a society work, a civilization work.

—Vince Lombardi

Background

This story is about how I resorted to some creative insubordination to keep my sanity during unproductive meetings. I was on my way to my twentieth unproductive meeting when I ran into my friend and colleague Rosemary. She looked at me and said, "I'd rather be going anywhere than to this meeting. I have so much to do, and you know this will be four hours of waste." I agreed, and off we went. As the meeting droned on, my mind started to wander, and that was when the trouble began. As I looked around at all the faces, my eyes stopped on an individual. All of a sudden I felt my lips involuntarily spreading into a grin. The individual looked like a penguin. I couldn't believe my eyes. I looked around the group again, and this time I saw Elmer Fudd. Next I saw an owl, and on and on.

What a menagerie. It was the funniest experience I'd had at one of these meetings. This little game was a well-kept secret. One day after a particularly boring meeting, Rosemary said, "Carol, at the last four meetings you seemed to be enjoying yourself. Surely you aren't enjoying the meetings?" I smiled and said, "Believe it or not, Rose, I am." She said, "How can this be? Am I missing something?" I told her she was, and that if I revealed my newfound technique to her, she could never tell anyone. When I told her what I was doing, she looked aghast. I encouraged her to try it. She let me know that it wasn't an option, and I dropped it right there. At the next meeting, we weren't 20 minutes into the agenda when the boredom set in. I began my game. My eyes caught Rosemary's. She was on the verge of slipping into craziness. I mouthed the word *owl*. She quickly looked down. Five minutes later, I saw her staring at the owl with a smile spreading across her lips. Meetings were never boring for us again.

What's the point of this story? It took a lot of creative energy and concentrated effort to play this game. Once we learned how to play, we did it with gusto. Just think of all that energy and gusto that could have been put to use had the person in charge of the meeting known how to make meetings work.

Did You Know

- The psychological reasons for meetings are a need to feel part of a group; a need for a sense of togetherness, trust, and belonging; a need to ease the loneliness and burden of responsibility; and a need to develop a sense of commitment.
- A researcher in the area of team performance estimates that the cost of time lost due to ineffective meetings amounts to $800,000 per year for every 1,000 employees.
- Most meetings are run according to some version of parliamentary procedure, which dates back to the nineteenth century.
- It's time to update how we deal with our changing environment when we get together in meetings.
- Most people have had little or no formal training in how to conduct or participate in meetings.

#68. Preventive Medicine

Ask the team members to share what they know about having productive meetings. Have the recorder record the main points. Let the discussion go on for about 10 or 15 minutes. Write the following statements on the blackboard or chart paper for all to see:

Before the meeting we need to:

At the beginning of the meeting we need to:

During the meeting we need to:

At the end of the meeting we need to:

Ask the team members to suggest items or ideas under each heading that they think will help them have productive meetings. Again, the recorder records the information. Once the information has been gathered, team members discuss how and what they need to do to be sure these things get done.

Materials You Will Need

several pieces of chart paper

a colored marker

masking tape

#69. What's Up, Doc?

Ask all team members to visit another team during one of *its* meetings. They must first ask permission of the team being observed and say that they want to observe a team in action to learn about effective team meetings. The person or persons visiting are only to record things that they liked. They are to bring this information to their team and discuss how they could use this information to make their team meetings more effective.

Do not allow gossip. Gossip defeats the purpose of the visit and causes trouble within the organization.

Materials You Will Need

#70. These Are a Must

Place the following chart on the wall:

These are a must:
Agendas
Minutes
Evaluation

Tell the team that in a productive meeting, these three items have to be present. Ask the team members to work in pairs for the next two weeks researching one of these items. In other words, if two of the team members choose to work on AGENDAS, they would find sample agendas they could share with the team. They would also talk to other people who have created agendas and find out a good way to set them, read about agendas in one of the reference books listed in this book and report back, and so on. After two weeks, bring the team back together and lead them in a sharing session. Have them report about all three areas. Then lead them in a discussion about how they would use this information in the most productive way. Make sure a recorder records the suggestions so team members can use them later when they develop plans for having success-ful meetings.

Materials You Will Need

any materials the pairs collect while doing their research

#71. Dear Teammate

Lead a discussion about what it takes to have an effective team meeting. Distribute to each team member one of the following index cards:

Dear Teammate:
Our team has a problem. At the meetings we seem to be going in different directions at the same time.

Dear Teammate:
We seem to be having a problem. Our team can never decide what topic or issue to discuss.

Dear Teammate:
I hope you can help us. We seem to have a leader who rubber stamps all the decisions. He thinks he's being collaborative but he's not. Help!

Dear Teammate:
Our team is very vocal with a lot of ideas. Sometimes we get so many ideas we can't remember all of them. What is our problem?

Dear Teammate:
I'm going crazy. We keep going over the same old ideas again and again.

Dear Teammate:
Our team never knows from one meeting to the next what we're going to do. Why?

Dear Teammate:
I don't know how long I can attend the team meetings and not say anything. I can't hear, can't see, it's too stuffy in the room, and it's cold. Brrrrr, help me.

Dear Teammate:
Our team comes up with good suggestions, but we aren't sure if we have the power to make decisions. Should we just make decisions or what?

SOURCE: Reprinted from Dave Francis and Don Young, *Improving Work Groups: A Practical Manual for Team Building,* San Diego, CA: Pfeiffer & Company, 1979. Used with permission.

Ask each team member to share his or her card with the rest of the team. The team discusses the possible reason or reasons for the problem and effective ways to deal with it. After members read the cards, ask if anyone would like to write a DEAR TEAMMATE card. If so, give the team a few minutes to write questions, and then ask members to share the problems and work through the same process to solve the problem. Ask the team to spend about five minutes discussing how to use this activity to make team meetings more effective.

Materials You Will Need

1 set of DEAR TEAMMATE cards

extra index cards

#72. Can You Take the Heat?

Share the Meetings Questionnaire (see the figure on the next page) with the team members. Tell them that after they have met four or five times, they will complete the questionnaire. Assure them that what they write on it will remain anonymous. After the fourth or fifth meeting, remind the team members to bring the questionnaire to the next meeting. Record the results on a large chart. Lead the members in a discussion about what they need to work on.

Materials You Will Need

1 copy of the Meetings Questionnaire per team member

1 piece of chart paper

a colored marker

masking tape

	4 True (Usually)	2 Sometimes	0 Not True (Seldom)
1. The purposes of our meetings are not defined.			
2. We do not decide what we want to achieve by the end of the meeting.			
3. People do not prepare sufficiently for our meetings.			
4. We seldom review our progress during meetings.			
5. We do not allocate meeting time well.			
6. Ideas and views often are lost or forgotten.			
7. We do not decide which agenda items have priority.			
8. We allocate equal amounts of time to trivia and important issues.			
9. People lose concentration and attention.			
10. Sometimes there are several meetings when there should be one.			
11. We do not review and confirm what has been agreed upon and how those decisions will be activated.			
12. The purposes of our meetings are not defined.			

Reprinted from Dave Francis and Don Young, *Improving Work Groups: A Practical Manual for Team Building*, San Diego, CA: Pfeiffer & Company, 1979. Used with permission.

Meetings Questionnaire

Instructions: Read the three scored headings and use them to evaluate each statement. Choose *one* score (4, 2, or 0) that corresponds to your opinion of how the statement applies to your meetings. Write the score in the appropriate blank.

FOR THE COMMITTED: IT MAKES ME WANT TO SHOUT!

By design and by talent we were a team of specialists, and like a team of specialists in any field our performance depended both on individual excellence and on how well we worked together. None of us had to strain to understand what we had to do to complement each other's specialties; it was simply a fact, and we all tried to figure out ways to make our combination more effective.

—Bill Russell

Background

Not long ago I was asked to spend a day and a half with 30 teams that needed help in learning how to work together. We spent much of the time learning how to design effective meetings. As I finished the training, I couldn't help wondering if anything I had taught would transfer to the teachers' world of work. I didn't have long to wonder, because I was invited to sit in on their first team meeting, which, unbeknownst to me, was that very afternoon. I crossed my fingers, held my breath, and waited.

The principal entered, gave the signal that the meeting was to begin, and started. One of the teachers raised her hand and said, "Mr. Principal, I have just been to a training session on how to have effective meetings. I would like to share some information with you and wonder if any of my colleagues would join me." The principal looked a bit shocked, but as all the other team members' hands went up, he acquiesced. For the next hour they shared ideas about setting agendas, dialogue, problem solving, and so on. When they finished, the administrator said, "Sounds like I should have been at that training. I tell you what: let's adjourn. No use having the meeting I planned. It's really my meeting and not a team meeting. Let's think of all the stuff we've learned and set the agenda for the next meeting." Believe it or not, a loud cheer went up from the team. The principal won a lot of respect that day, and I believe a team was born. It made me want to shout, "It can be done, it can be done!"

Did You Know

- Meetings are an intensive way of involving others in solving problems and making decisions.
- Two questions to judge the success of a meeting are What happened? and What problems did we solve?
- Teams can learn to think reflectively, creatively, and productively.
- It's tempting to overload an agenda.
- Meetings are good for generating ideas, sharing information, and making shared decisions.

#73. The Meeting of the Future

Tell the team to fantasize for a moment. The year is 2050. The team has been asked to design the perfect meeting. It is the meeting that will be the model for training the rest of the organization in how to have quality meetings. Your team is to design the perfect meeting room facility, the latest in technology, ways to facilitate time for meetings, length of meetings with breaks that facilitate learning, and anything else that will ensure quality meetings.

After the team has spent 30 or 40 minutes designing the meeting of the future, it comes back to reality. Ask team members to look at what they have created. Focus on what parts of their fantasy they can make come true. Lead them in developing an action plan to get what they need to have the best meetings.

Materials You Will Need

chart paper

assorted colored markers

masking tape

#74. It's Simply Got to Be There

Ask the team members to volunteer to learn about the following topics:

problem solving

decision making

conflict management

consensus

agenda setting

discussion methods

meeting evaluation

The team members can work alone, in pairs, or in groups, as long as everyone is working on a topic. Have them spend three weeks gathering information. The Further Readings in this book are excellent resources. Other ways to learn about the topic are workshops, college classes, human resources departments, other people, consultants, and audio or videotapes.

The team sets a date when everyone is to share information. Once the information is shared, the team decides on a procedure. For example, all teams need to have a problem-solving model to use. The person, pair, or group that is to bring back information on this topic may share two or three different models. The team then chooses a model that best suits it.

Materials You Will Need

Whatever the person, pair, or group needs to have in order to present topic information

7

Creating
Agendas

Anything less than a conscious commitment to the important is an unconscious commitment to the unimportant.

—Stephen R. Covey

Not long ago a superintendent of a large school district asked me to facilitate a meeting. This meeting was very important because the outcome might very well determine the success of three years of intensive work done by members of the high school who were trying to effect a major restructuring. I felt very strongly that this meeting should be viewed as the superintendent's meeting, so I wanted to be clear that he was determining the meeting agenda, not me. I was the facilitator, the one to keep things safe and orderly. So I did not design an agenda. After all, it was the superintendent's meeting, not mine. Right? Thirty minutes before the meeting was to take place, the superintendent arrived and suggested the two of us meet for a "few" minutes to discuss the meeting. I discovered very quickly he did not have a set agenda, and like it or not, it was going to be up to me to set the stage, cite the objectives, and keep things moving. We agreed that if any yelling or inappropriate

113

behavior occurred, we would end the meeting. I felt very confident that this enthusiastic leader and I could "conquer" the world. In we went with no written agenda. The first 30 minutes were good, but from there it was all downhill. All I know is that I started the meeting sounding so good and in control. The superintendent got up and began talking with enthusiasm. Next thing I knew, there were lots of questions. I was still "good and in control." I quickly realized that I had to protect the superintendent from things getting out of hand, so I stepped forward with my best facilitator voice and set up a process for asking questions. But when the superintendent began to respond, World War III began. Here's the funny thing. There were only three people in the opposing army. The rest were silent. Then there was the superintendent and me. But the three in the opposing army were wild. I finally said, "Stop! We can't go forward, because we agreed to follow the code of conduct and that is not happening. We will end this meeting and try again at another time." There was DEAD silence. People were stunned. No one moved. All of a sudden one of the participants said, "Look, no one is leaving. Why can't we take this opportunity to talk and see if we can move forward?" I looked down at a blank piece of paper where there was NO agenda. I had no plan, I had violated my cardinal rule to never facilitate a meeting without a plan. This meeting will forever be etched in my memory not only as the worst meeting I ever conducted but as a meeting whose failure was all my fault and could have been prevented with proper agenda design.

The story above should never have happened. In his book *101 Ways to Make Meetings Active,* Mel Silberman (1999) says, "The preparation of an agenda is the first step in planning any meeting. An active agenda communicates to participants how to prepare for and participate in an upcoming meeting." Donald Hackett and Charles Martin (1993), coauthors of *Facilitation Skills for Team Leaders,* say that the success of a meeting depends upon what happens in preparation of the meeting.

Over the years, as I coach teams to a performing stage, some of the traps they have fallen into and have to get out of are as follows:

- Team members attending the meeting don't know the purpose.
- The outcome of the meeting is not clear.
- One person controls the meeting.
- Too much time is spent on an item or issue.
- Team members on the agenda are not prepared.
- Team members running the meetings are not prepared.
- There is no data collection as to whether the meetings are productive or achieving their goal.
- The team jumps from one topic to another.
- The team does not stay focused on the agenda.
- Team members misbehave.

I am sure you could add many more items to this list, but these seem to be the most common. The bad news is that these problems occur because teams do not develop all the components of teaming listed in this book. The good news is that one of the quickest solutions to get out of one of these traps, or to keep from falling into the trap to begin with, is to have a well-crafted and executed agenda.

Oriel Incorporated is an organization that provides consulting and training designed to help systems increase their performance. They suggest that there are three stages to plan for when preparing for a meeting. The chart below is an example of the three stages.

As I was listing the three stages one needs to plan for to get ready for a meeting, my failure to do *any* of the *before* stage jumps out at me. I could not get the meeting back on the right path because I did not have a clear idea of the outcome the superintendent wanted, what the potential problems were, or who had been invited. I find myself turning red with embarrassment at my poor judgment and lack of planning. Every problem that occurred that fateful day could have been prevented by a well-crafted and executed agenda. In order that you will not have to experience the horror and sense of failure that I did, I have designed this chapter to give you an opportunity to go through a series of exercises that will ensure your agendas are well crafted and executed.

BEFORE MEETING	DURING MEETING	AFTER MEETING
(The planning stage)	(The starting, conducting, and closing stage)	(Following up)
• Clarify purpose and outcomes of the meeting • Identify meeting participants • Choose methods for accomplishing the meeting's purpose and outcomes • Develop the agenda with starting and ending times for each item • Send agenda to participants early • Arrange room and equipment	• Start with a warm-up • Review the agenda • Set or review ground rules • Clarify roles • Cover one agenda item at a time • Establish an appropriate pace • Open discussions • Maintain focus of discussions • Manage participation • Check decisions • Close discussions • Summarize decisions • Agree on action items • Draft agenda for next meeting • Evaluate the meeting • Thank participants	• Write and distribute meeting minutes • File the agenda, minutes, and other key documents • Carry out assignments • Set a time for premeeting planning

Simple Things to Do:
What's Up, Doc?

We need objectives. We need focus and direction. Most of
all, we need the sense of accomplishment that comes from
achieving what we set out to do.

—Leon Tec, MD

Background

I have been in education for 41 years. I have two degrees and
a number of endorsements in early childhood education, special
education, and administration. I have also taken hundreds of
hours in staff development, attended preconference sessions at
many of the national conferences, taken four- to five-day training courses, and so on. This is not to mention the thousands of
dollars I have invested in my own professional library, videos,
and now CDs and DVDs to continue my quest to be a lifelong
learner. During all of this education, I never heard anyone talk
about the importance of preparing an agenda. No one alluded to
the fact that a well-planned agenda indicates a lot about one's
understanding of how to facilitate a good meeting. Heaven for-
bid if anyone hinted that an agenda might be the saving grace of
a meeting with unruly participants. In fact, as I began collecting
agendas from anyone who would part with theirs, the only comment ever made was, "You can have a copy, but it's not very
good." It was almost as if they knew it should be better but
really didn't know how to make it better. Saying they were sorry
was supposed to make it okay. Mentor after mentor taught
me wonderful things but never taught me how to develop an
agenda or mentioned its importance. Then one year I met
Dr. Rosemary Lambie. Dr. Lambie taught at Virginia Commonwealth University. She asked me to apply for a job on one of her
grants. I did, got the job, and started working with her. It was
Dr. Lambie who taught me the value of good planning. Her
agendas were so detailed that from time to time I secretly wondered about her. She had a memory that was incredible. When I
would prepare the agenda, she would go through it and say

things like, "Have you planned what you will do when no one shows up on time? What will you do about people who have a part on the agenda are unprepared? What strategy have you determined would be the most effective for consensus building? Who is doing what?" She was and still is the most outstanding planning expert I have ever met. I learned more from her than all my years in college. She encouraged me to read and study about quality meetings. I have spent the last 10 years doing so.

Did You Know

- The facilitator is typically responsible for the structure of the meeting.
- Sometimes a rough draft of an agenda can be created on the spot.
- If an agenda has not been prepared, spend the first five minutes of the meeting creating an agenda on a flip chart.
- The preparation of the agenda is the first step in planning.
- A printed agenda can be used with special touches that can lighten up the meeting.

#75. The Spotlight Is on You

This activity is for the team leader to use if an agenda has not been developed ahead of time. The team leader tells the group they are going to take five minutes to develop the agenda so people will know what the purpose is and what is going to happen. The leader turns to a chart that has been prepared 10 minutes before the meeting and fills in the blanks with the team. The chart has the following information on it:

MEETING PURPOSE:

GROUND RULES:

TOPICS WITH TIME ALLOTMENTS:

MEETING EVALUATION:

Once the information is on the chart, the leader tells the team to take a minute to reflect on the agenda and see if there is anything they need to add or clarify before the meeting actually gets started.

Materials You Will Need

poster paper with the agenda headings

a colored marker

#76. Quick and Easy

Before the meeting, prepare a chart with headings as shown on the example below. Place it on the easel and ask the team to give their input as they help develop the next meeting agenda. Briefly remind them of the meaning of the categories.

Quick & Easy

Trust Activity		5 Minutes
Quick Items	Major Items	Minor Items
Example: Paperwork that has to be in the office 5 minutes	Example: How to develop an interdisciplinary unit 30 minutes	Example: Where are kids going to sit in the assembly? 15 minutes
FEEDBACK: COACH DECIDES 5 minutes		

- The Trust Activity is just a short process to help them unwind from the day or to get to know each other a little better.
- The Quick Items are things that will only take a minute or two to complete. Examples would be due dates for items to be turned in to the office, permission slips for field trips, or just reminders of things that are happening in the school that will affect the team.

- Major Items are things that take time to discuss and process for solutions. Usually there is only one item in this column because it is important not to overload an agenda. It is better to put less on the agenda and get it all done than to constantly overload it and feel frustrated because nothing gets completed.
- The Minor Items column comprises items that take more time to complete than the Quick Items column but not as long as the Major Items column. There may be two items taking about five minutes each, such as report card information and textbook sharing.
- The last section is usually done by the team coach. The coach plans an activity that is intended to give the team feedback on how they are functioning as a team. It is designed for growth and development of the team. For some ideas, turn to Chapter 9 on feedback and select an activity.

Materials You Will Need

a copy of the Quick and Easy Agenda

colored markers

#77. Sealed With a Kiss

When a meeting is especially important and the facilitator has been given the responsibility of designing the agenda, ask a few of the team members to serve as "guides." Give the guides ahead of time a copy of the agenda and a list of questions such as the following:

Do the topics on the agenda support the objectives of the meeting?

Are there agenda items that need to be added?

Are the processes being used to facilitate the agenda items the best ones to use?

Do the time frames for each item seem appropriate?

What do you know that I don't know about some of the topics on the agenda?

What do you approve of and why?

What do you not approve of and why?

Once the facilitator has received information from the guides, ask them for their support, redo the agenda using their suggestions, and ask for their approval.

Materials You Will Need

a copy of the drafted agenda

#78. Put It in the Parking Lot

Tell the team that one of the best ways to get an agenda done for the next meeting is to use a technique called the Parking Lot. The Parking Lot is a large sheet of paper with a large circle drawn in the middle. As the meeting is being conducted and team members bring up items, issues, or concerns that are not on the agenda, they are placed in the Parking Lot. At the end of the meeting, the facilitator tells the team that they need to go to the Parking Lot and choose the items that they would like to put on the agenda for the next meeting. This would be a good time to use the Quick and Easy agenda found in Activity #77. The Parking Lot is a professional way to honor team members' concerns and yet at the same time keep the team focused. The team facilitator uses the information from the Parking Lot to design the agenda. The agenda is distributed a week ahead of time if possible but not later than 24 hours.

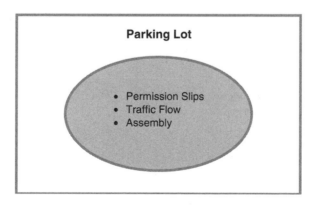

Materials You Will Need

poster paper

a colored marker

#79. Lighten Up

From time to time, teams get discouraged by the number of meetings they have to attend. Sometimes the meeting topic is boring but necessary. Why not lighten up the meeting with printed material—the agenda. Ninety-eight percent of the world responds to visual stimuli. This activity can be done by the person who completes the final draft of the agenda.

Materials You Will Need

a final draft of the agenda

whatever you do to lighten up the agenda such as cartoons, quotes, and so on

#80. Bingo Boogie

The team leader tells the team that they are going to have a very different-looking agenda for the meeting. Each member is given a bingo card with *some* of the agenda items in the various boxes. All the cards are the same except one. *One* card has *all* the topics. The leader begins the meeting, and as he or she talks about an item, the team members cross the item off. The person who gets all the items crossed off calls out "BINGO" and wins a prize.

Halloween Party	Team Analysis	New Data System
Referral Slips	Schedule	Report Cards

(Winning Card)

Halloween Party	New Data System	Referral Slips
Report Cards	Team Analysis	Popcorn

Materials You Will Need

copies of bingo cards that have most, but not all, of the meeting topics as well as one or two incorrect topics

a copy of a bingo card that has all the meeting topics

a prize for the winner

THINGS THAT TAKE EFFORT: OUT TO LUNCH

Beware of the man who won't be bothered with details.

—William Feather

Background

I really cut my teeth on the concept of teaming during my work with middle schools. In my career I have probably trained 3,000 middle school teachers, and the one thing they consistently told me was that they really did not see developing an agenda as important. When asked why, the usual comments were "It takes too long. We meet three times a week, which is too many agendas. Who cares? There are only four of us, so why have all that detail?" I spent years trying to sell the idea and also to help them see that it is not hard to write agendas once they learn how. They graciously tolerated me, but one day a younger teacher stayed after the session and said, "Mrs. Scearce, we really like you, but this agenda thing is just not for us. We know you're going to expect to see them when you visit, but let me express our feelings in your generation's terminology: "Agendas are out to lunch!!" All of a sudden I had an aha moment. I said, "Oh, you mean they're just not cool?" "Well," he said, "it's just the way you do them that's not cool." I looked at him with a stunned look on my face and said, "You mean if you could design your own format you might be willing to do them?" He said, "Yeah, like, could we work smarter, not harder?" That was a teachable moment for me. From that day on, I taught them the components of an agenda, did a good sell job on why each part was important and how it could help them, and then I said, "Your team has 20 minutes to design a format specifically for your team." Here's the weird thing—all of a sudden, they couldn't wait to design formats.

Then they began to share them and take the best from each. Needless to say, I don't have trouble with agendas anymore.

Did You Know

- The preparation of the agenda is the first step in planning.
- All agenda items should support the meeting objectives.
- An agenda is a plan or a map for a meeting.
- An agenda helps to plan effective strategy for achieving goals.
- The more clearly goals and objectives are defined, the easier it is to decide upon strategy.

#81. Which Number Will It Be?

Have the team leader explain to the team that an important part of working smarter and not harder is to be well focused and well planned. Share each of the following three agenda formats and samples and ask the team members to take a day to reflect on what they have heard. Tell them to be ready to share their thoughts on the format they would like to use at the next team meeting.

Agenda Format Number 1

The team leader explains that the top of the format is a quick way to keep up with the roles of the team members so there is no confusion as to who is responsible for what. The attendance line is there so that the team will remember to get information to the people who could not attend the meeting. The date is there to be able to record the amount of meeting time that occurred for documentation.

Next the team leader explains briefly each of the columns on the agenda format.

The TIME column allows the team to monitor the group's use of time and to point out how much time remains for a topic. If the group is not finished at the allotted time, the team facilitator asks the team if they want to continue discussing the subject or move on.

The TOPIC is the specific problem issue or solution that is to be dealt with during that time. Knowing the topics helps the team members to come focused and prepared. It also helps the facilitator to know when the team is off the subject.

The PERSON is the person on the team who will be responsible for a specific agenda topic. This helps the team check for equality in participation. On a high-performing team, all the members are accountable. One person does not do all the work.

The METHOD is the way the topic is going to be presented and what process would be used if there was to be a discussion or problem-solving activity. This ensures that there is a plan and that the team does not operate on a *ready, fire, aim* basis.

The OUTCOME is what the team wants to produce or have happen at the meeting in regard to the topic. This component ensures accountability.

The team leader gives the members about two minutes to reflect on what he or she has said and then asks for clarifying questions. Once the questions have been cleared up, the team leader refers the team to AGENDA FORMAT NUMBER 2. Tell the team that this one is similar to the first format with two exceptions. Direct them to the top of the form and tell them that this one has a DATE section, but in addition has the days of the week so they can circle the day they are meeting. The second addition to this format is the column titled RESULT. This column makes note of what happens to each topic in relation to the OUTCOME. It serves as simple minutes for the meeting.

The team leader gives the members two minutes to reflect on FORMAT 2 and then asks for clarifying questions. Once the questions have been cleared up, the team leader refers the team to AGENDA FORMAT NUMBER 3.

The team leader explains that this format is similar to #1 and #2 but keeps the team focused on five areas. Those areas are as follows:

1. Student Issues are anything about students that would pertain to the team or where team input would be helpful.

2. Curriculum Issues are issues that might involve standards, interdisciplinary teaching, homework, and so on.

3. Adult Issues are issues that involve team members or other staff that are involved with the team in some way such as the counselor or physical education teacher.

4. Have To's are things that come from the administration that we may not be vested in but we have to do.

5. Nitty Gritty is anything that doesn't fall under any of the above.

The team leader gives two minutes for reflection and then asks for clarifying questions. Divide the team into pairs. Each person chooses a number, a 1 or a 2. Partner #1 selects one of the three formats for agendas and reteaches it to his or her partner. If there is any confusion or questions, it is at this time that the team leader clears it up. Partner #2 selects one of the formats and reteaches his or her partner. The format that is left is reviewed together. Once the team members have a good understanding of each of the formats, the leader tells them to take them home and reflect on them. Team members are reminded that at the next meeting, they will decide on a format that the team would like to use.

Materials

copies of the three agenda formats and examples

pen or pencil

paper for taking notes

AGENDA FORMAT NUMBER 1

Meeting Schedule

Leader/Facilitator: _____   Coach: _____

Recorder: _____   P.A.: _____

Attendance: _____

Date: _____

Time	Topic	Person	Method	Outcome

AGENDA FORMAT NUMBER 1
Example

Meeting Schedule

Leader/Facilitator: Jonathan   Coach: Brenda

Recorder: Kathy   P.A.: Donna

Attendance: _____

Date: _____

Time	Topic	Person	Method	Outcome
12:45–12:50	Halloween Party	All	Round-Robin Discussion	Letter to parents Time frame Food arrangements
12:50–12:55	Halloween Video	All	Four-Step Discussion Method	Where shown Title
12:50–1:00	Halloween Costumes	All	Popcorn Discussion	What's acceptable
1:00–1:10	Field Trips	All	Round-Robin Discussion	Final decision Ellen to make reservations
1:10–1:15	Summarize decisions	Jonathan	Chart to list decisions	Final decisions
1:15–1:20	Coaching Comments	Brenda	Productivity Chart	Did well!
1:20–1:23	Draft next agenda	All	Discussion	Topics for next meeting

AGENDA FORMAT NUMBER 2

Team Meeting

Leader: _____   Coach: _____

Recorder: _____   Materials: _____   Facilitator: _____

Date: Monday   Tuesday
Wednesday   Thursday   Friday

Time	Topic	Person	Method	Outcome	Result

AGENDA FORMAT NUMBER 2 Example

Team Meeting

Leader: Carol   Coach: David

Recorder: Lori   Materials: Facilitator: Jeff

Date: Monday Tuesday Wednesday Thursday Friday

Time	Topic	Person	Method	Outcome	Result
1:00–1:10	Detention	Carol	Direct report from data	To determine if sixth-grade Team A has enough students attending detention to declare it a problem	Team A discovered the problem wasn't a large number of students in detention *but* the same students attend a large number of times
1:10–1:30	Interdisciplinary Unit	David	PCI	To determine what our next action steps will be	Discovered the unit lends itself to art & music, so we could invite them to participate
1:30–1:40	Team Analysis	Jeff	Checklist from Teaming Book	To validate that we are performing at a high level as a team	The team scored high on team assessment except in one area, and that was beginning right on time

AGENDA FORMAT NUMBER 3

Agenda

Time	Topic	Person	Method	Outcome	Result
	Student Issues				
	Curriculum Issues				
	Adult Issues				
	Have To's				
	Nitty Gritty				

AGENDA FORMAT NUMBER 3 Example

Agenda

Time	Topic	Person	Method	Outcome	Result
1:00–1:15	Student Issues Mike S.	Pat	MAPS PROCESS	Every team member input into the five categories of MAPS in order to develop a whole picture of Mike—where he is and where we want him to be at the end of the year	The team has a holistic picture of Mike. We reached a consensus on goals for him. Each of us is going to develop a plan in our content area and report to team.
1:15–1:25	Curriculum Issues First Integrated Unit	John	Web Brainstorm	Ten or more ideas to begin discussing as a possible integrated unit. Must tie into NY standards.	We only came up with five ideas but all agreed that they were all good ideas.
1:25–1:35	Adult Issues Everyone not present at team meetings	Carol	Talk around Using team attendance from Post-it note suggestions rated by group	To come up with a solution, collaboratively developed, that will get all our team members to the meetings.	We agreed that if we started meeting five minutes later, it would solve the problem.
1:35–1:40	Have To's Field trip dates to office by Friday	Bob	Vote on three choices	Select one date to send to office	Voted—chose April 10
1:40–1:45	Nitty Gritty Halloween Video	John	Popcorn Discussion	To choose one video to show	Didn't get to this

#82. What's a Keeper?

The team leader brings copies of all three samples of agenda formats from Activity #81. He distributes them to each of the team members. He then puts the PCI Chart below on a flip chart. The team members look at Sample #1 and give feedback using the PCI Chart on that agenda format. Go through all three of the formats and then decide which format the team wants to use. The team may choose to create its own format.

P	C	I
What are the positive points of this format?	What are the concerns with this format?	What interesting data can we collect from this format?

Materials You Will Need

> poster paper with the PCI Chart drawn on it
>
> a colored marker
>
> copies of agenda formats 1, 2, and 3 for each person

FOR THE COMMITTED: THIS IS MY FINAL ANSWER

Every time you have a task before you, examine it carefully, take exact measure of what is expected of you. Then make your plan and, in order to execute it properly, create for yourself a method, never improvise.

—Marshal Ferdinand Foch

Background

I am working with a school system on a very complicated organizational change. We have been meeting once a month for the last three years. I have a team of about 40 or more educators, which is a large team. One of the things I do consistently is follow the rules on agendas. I choose an agenda format that is detailed, because the process is fairly complicated, and since I live in another state, I want to be sure we were communicating on a high level. Every month I send a letter that usually has an article about the change we are working through and an uplifting quote that pertains to the courage it takes to change, and then I attach a detailed agenda. This information is sent out three weeks ahead of time. I must admit that sometimes I don't want to go to all the trouble, and I even wonder if anyone really reads the material. After a year and a half on the project, I became ill and had to take a two-month leave of absence. The good news is that the project kept going without me. When I returned, a number of people came up and said they were glad I was back. In fact, so many made the same comment that I felt I needed to acknowledge their support publicly during the meeting. When I finished commending them for continuing without me and thanked them for missing me, one of the team members raised his hand and said, "Do you know what we missed the most? We missed the letter of support and getting our agenda. We didn't get anything but a notice of the meeting while you were gone." Being a teacher, I never want to miss an opportunity for learning, so I asked, "Why was all of that so important?" The reply from one teacher was "I loved knowing what we were going to do, how we were going to do it, when we would be finished, and *best* of all, I have *all* of my agendas. As we finish each item, I check off the Outcome column. It gives me a strong sense that all the time I'm taking from my classroom is worth it because we're accomplishing something. Not to mention I have a lot of great quotes for my file."

It was at that moment that I knew all the time and effort I put into the letters, quotes, and agendas were worth it. From all the literature that I have read, the experts tell you that people want agendas, they want to know what is going on, and it's worth the time. But how often do you hear a person actually make the comment I was able to hear? It was such a powerful case for crafting and executing agendas. I rest my case—just do it!

Did You Know

- Teams exist to achieve results.
- Effective team achievements require clear objectives.
- A well-crafted agenda provides structures that guide the meeting.
- An effective team sets high standards of achievement.
- Agendas can be used for data collection.

#83. This Is Our Final Answer

The team leader distributes the copy of the Oriel meeting flowchart to each team member. Tell the group that this agenda and meeting format has been developed by an organization that is known for the quality of its work with team building and quality meetings.

Ask the team to use the next eight minutes to read the meeting format and mark it as follows:

Put an * next to any suggestion they like and want to use

Put an × next to any suggestion they think is not necessary

Put a ? next to anything they need explained or want to talk about

When time is up, the team leader leads a discussion on each of the marks. The team members listen to what their teammates say and create the way they want their agendas to look and how they want their meetings to be structured. The team recorder records the team suggestions on chart paper.

Materials

1 copy of the Oriel meeting flowchart per person

pencils

chart paper

MEETING PROCESS FLOWCHART

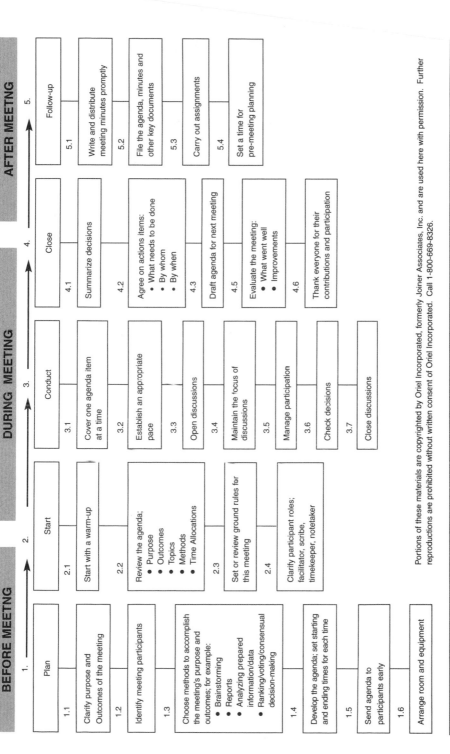

BEFORE MEETNG

1. Plan

1.1 Clarify purpose and Outcomes of the meeting

1.2 Identify meeting participants

1.3 Choose methods to accomplish the meeting's purpose and outcomes; for example:
● Brainstorming
● Reports
● Analyzing prepared information/data
● Ranking/voting/consensual decision-making

1.4 Develop the agenda; set starting and ending times for each time

1.5 Send agenda to participants early

1.6 Arrange room and equipment

2. Start

2.1 Start with a warm-up

2.2 Review the agenda;
● Purpose
● Outcomes
● Topics
● Methods
● Time Allocations

2.3 Set or review ground rules for this meeting

2.4 Clarify participant roles; facilitator, scribe, timekeeper, notetaker

DURING MEETING

3. Conduct

3.1 Cover one agenda item at a time

3.2 Establish an appropriate pace

3.3 Open discussions

3.4 Maintain the focus of discussions

3.5 Manage participation

3.6 Check decisions

3.7 Close discussions

4. Close

4.1 Summarize decisions

4.2 Agree on actions items:
● What needs to be done
  • By whom
  • By when

4.3 Draft agenda for next meeting

4.5 Evaluate the meeting:
● What went well
● Improvements

4.6 Thank everyone for their contributions and participation

AFTER MEETNG

5. Follow-up

5.1 Write and distribute meeting minutes promptly

5.2 File the agenda, minutes and other key documents

5.3 Carry out assignments

5.4 Set a time for pre-meeting planning

From Peter Scholtes, Brian Joiner, Barbara Streibel, *The Team Handbook, Third Edition*. © 2006 Oriel Incorporated. All Rights Reserved.

#84. What's It All About?

The activity takes place at the end of each grading period. The team gathers all of its agendas in order to analyze the data. The recorder makes a six-column chart on a piece of poster paper, chalkboard or a white board. The categories of the columns correspond to the agenda format the team is using. An example might be the following column headings:

TOPIC

TIME

PERSON

METHOD

OUTCOME

RESULTS

The team members look through all of the agendas and list under the Topic column all the topics they have focused on for the grading period. They look at Time and add up the total amount of time they have spent on specific topics. For example, they may see that they have agenda items that fall under a category of discipline, and they notice they have spent a total of six hours talking about discipline. When they get to the Results column, they notice that they have not achieved satisfactory results with the topic of discipline. What they discover is that they have spent a lot of time talking and complaining but not coming up with a solution that gets rid of the problem. Another example might be that they recognize they have spent a lot of time on the topic of homework, and the results show that the number of homework problems have decreased. The data analysis comes from the six components of the agenda. It enables the team to do the following:

Set goals for the next grading period

Adjust the way the team works together

Share data with administration or others

Discuss the pros and cons of working together

Celebrate successes

Materials You Will Need

copies of all the agendas for the time period from which you are collecting data

poster paper to make chart with the agenda columns

colored markers

8

Using Process

The workshop was packed. No seats were left. One hundred teachers, principals, superintendents, board members, and even a few high school students were in the audience to learn tools for solving problems. I spent two days teaching them everything I knew about finding root causes, using data, learning how to have effective discussions, methods for solving problems, and more. At the end of the first day, I was exhausted from modeling, giving them real problems and letting them practice, observing them, and giving feedback. That night I went to bed at 7:00 p.m. The second day began. People were enthusiastic. They got right into the active participation. At 2:30 p.m. I looked at the clock and knew I had given my all. It was now time to get feedback from them as to the usefulness of the tools they had come to learn. I got an A+ on presentation, material, and knowledge. My chest began to puff out a little although I was sure not to let anyone notice. Now for the most informative part—the comments and suggestions. I knew they were going to be reinforcing. Let me just put some of them in print for you to read.

- Most engaging workshop I have attended, but there is no way I could take the time to use the tools to solve problems.
- If Carol would come to my system and do these, it would be good. No one will listen to me.
- Good, but could have been done in one day.

> - *I could not help but enjoy the workshop, but what does this have to do with me? I teach kids.*
> - *Good tools but no time.*
> - *I liked the tools, but when do you use them?*
> - *Does my principal know these tools?*
> - *I liked the tools but am afraid to try because I might mess up.*
>
> *I can't explain how I felt. Even though there were many more positive comments about the usefulness of the tools, it was the comments above that stunned me. I realized I had done a good job presenting the tools, but I hadn't spent enough time helping people to buy into the pay value of using them. Pay value means "What's in it for me?" It's the motivation piece to anything that we do. If I had been able to show them why it was worth the time and effort to use process tools, they would have transferred them into their life. I learned a lot that day, reading those evaluations. It really doesn't matter if the workshop is great, or people say they love you, or they go on and on about your humor. If they don't see the value in what you're teaching, then time and money have been wasted. More important, people will go on trying to solve problems that impact students, using the same old tools they have always used, which is most often none. The story has a good ending. I added a major segment to the workshop on the uses and the value of using process tools to solve problems. I'm happy to report I'm getting a higher level of transfer from the workshop.*

This is an important story to share with anyone who is going to be involved in problem solving, solution design, and action plans, because without process, the results are usually dismal. People will fight the use of process because they encounter personality clashes, time wasters, and procedural wrangling. It is the role of the facilitator to convince the group of the value of using tools. The facilitator must have a well-stocked tool kit of techniques to suggest processes and assist teams as they attempt to focus on issues, generate ideas for solutions, make decisions, and develop action plans. It is through the use of process tools that the right atmosphere is created to enable the team to make good decisions and to develop solutions with an action plan that moves them toward success.

This chapter is designed to equip anyone who is responsible for problem solving with a well-stocked tool kit. All the suggestions in this chapter have been used by me on numerous occasions in various settings with success.

SIMPLE THINGS TO DO: WORLD WAR III

It is the greatest of all mistakes to do nothing because you can do only a little. Do what you can.

—Sydney Smith

People often tell me I have a special gift of being able to get people to open up and speak the truth without creating World War III. I am always amazed by this and ask them to give me specific feedback on what it is I do. I'm curious as to what they observe. They say things like "You have a way with humor that defuses things," or "There's something about your expressions," or "Your body language and your words are congruent and you just seem so relaxed and trustworthy." I could keep going here, but I think you get the point. Never has one person hit on the truth of what it is I do. So I'm going to tell you, because if you ever run into me, you'll know my secret. Whenever I go into a situation that I know is going to involve problem solving or conflict, I arm myself with tools. I spend hours thinking of a process I can suggest to get people talking and problem solving in a safe environment. Everyone has an opportunity to be heard first in a small group, and then I create a process for speaking out in the large group. The test I use before I settle on a process is a question: If anything could go wrong, what would it be? I then add a little creativity of my own to tweak the process so the problem will most likely not occur. This is the secret to any success. You see, I never want to be involved in starting World War III. I make sure my tool kit is bigger than anyone else's.

Did You Know

- Once obstacles and opportunities have been determined, you can plan to use specific process techniques that will often eliminate the obstacles and allow for the necessary opportunities.
- The process techniques you use will have an effect on people.
- Be ready to suggest a process technique.
- The group needs to be hard on issues and soft on people.

#85. Positives and Negatives

Ask each person on the team to fold a piece of paper into three columns. Label the first column P and tell the group to write under it "Positive impact of the problem/solution/issue." Label the second column C and tell the team to write under it "Concerns I have about the problem/solution/issue." Label the last column I and tell the group to write under it "Interesting things that might happen as a result of not dealing with the problem/solution/issue."

Give the team about five minutes to respond individually to the problem/solution and then have them share with the team, one column at a time. Once everyone has shared, have the team synthesize the responses on a piece of chart paper.

P	C	I
Positive impact of the problem/ solution/issue	Concerns I have about the problem/ solution/issue	Interesting things that might happen as a result of not dealing with the problem/ solution/issue

Materials You Will Need

chart paper

colored markers

individual sheets of paper

pencils

#86. What's the Focus?

This process technique is useful when team members need to read and discuss material such as data, research, or an article to gain understanding of a problem, issue, and/or solution. Ask the team members to use a pencil to mark the material using the following symbols:

\#   I knew this

!   This is good information because

?   Not sure what this means

−   I disagree because

Allow time for them to read silently and to mark their text. When time is up, ask team members to share information they marked with the number symbol (#) and the exclamation point (!). Next ask them to get into small groups to discuss the information marked with the question mark (?). If questions can't be answered in the small groups, then the team leader should share knowledge with the group. Last, have team members discuss material marked with the minus sign (−). The leader then gives Post-it notes to individual team members and asks that they suggest the next steps they would suggest to take in regard to the problem, issue, or solution. All of the next steps are collected and shared with the team. The team can do one of the following:

Select the next step suggestions they think are best, and generate a quick action plan.

Have the team leader take all the suggestions the team agreed on and decide on an action plan.

The team prioritizes the next steps in order of impact and creates an action plan.

Turn to activity #88 or #93 for action plan examples or use one that the team has used in the past.

Materials You Will Need

pencils

materials to be read

Post-it notes

white board to sketch out action plan

#87. Report Card

Use this process to elicit feedback from all team members without opening the meeting up to an extensive discussion. Give the team members a copy of the report card below and invite them to complete it with their thoughts about the identified problem, issue, or solution. Explain that the responses will be compiled and shared at the next team meeting and will be used in determining the next steps that will be taken.

REPORT CARD
Most Important
A Surprise
A New Question
A Point of Confusion
How does this problem, issue, or solution relate to your life?

#88. Action Plan

Action plans are analogous to lesson plans. There are many styles and formats that can be used to accomplish any number of purposes. It is my belief that the decision about what format to use should be driven by two questions: (1) How much time does the team have? (2) How much planning is required to effectively accomplish the defined task? Any action plan should be user friendly and should provide sufficient detail so that everyone understands how to implement the plan. The action plan listed below is a very simple one. The next two sections offer more detailed plan formats that can be used when solving complex problems or grappling with weighty issues and complicated solutions.

Simple Action Plan

WHO	WHAT	HOW	WHEN	WHERE
Person responsible	Step or outcome	Step-by-step plan	Date and time	Location
Ex.: Carol	Ex.: One-day workshop on teaching vocabulary	Ex.: Call literacy coach and develop plan	Ex.: Oct. 17, 2006	Ex.: Balboa Elem. School in teachers' meeting
		Share information with staff for feedback		
		Reserve faculty meeting room		
		Duplicate workshop material		
		Design evaluation		

THINGS THAT TAKE EFFORT: ME TOO!

Wisdom is the power to see, and the inclination to choose, the best and highest goal, together with the surest means of attaining it.

—J. I. Packer

Background

I received a call from an assistant superintendent who said, "Carol, we're having a big problem with a specific department. They have a new supervisor, and the teachers from the different schools have divided into two camps. One camp likes her and is trying to be cooperative, and the other side sabotages everything she does. To tell you the truth, this group has always been disagreeable." She went on to give me more history. Then she said, "Can you come and help us out? We have a half-day release time." I asked her what had been tried so far. She said she had talked to some of the teachers individually, which didn't work. They had had a group meeting, but that ended up as a shouting match. I asked her again what she had tried. She answered the same. Then she said, "I want to help them, and I want you to help us. The superintendent said he wants me to be sure you plan what you're going to do because he wants you to be successful." I responded to her, "Me too! You can rest assured that if I take the job, no one wants me to be more successful than me."

I told you this story for two reasons. First, did you notice that once the assistant superintendent had told me what she had tried, I asked her again, "What have you tried?" I was trying to find out what process tools she used when she met with the teachers as a group. She sat them in a room, started a dialogue, and thought they could talk. The bottom line—no process. She had good intentions but no tool kit of techniques to problem solve.

The second reason I told you this story is that they all wanted me to be a success because they needed a success. Let me say, there are no consultants alive who do not want success more than the people who have hired them. But to have success in problem solving, one has to use process techniques that are very carefully thought out, and the system has to allow time to identify the problem and solve the problem. Problems that are complicated cannot be worked out in an hour, or half a day, or—most of the time—even a day.

I chose to add process strategies in this second edition because I discovered over my 40 years in education that many teachers and administrators don't use any types of tools to solve problems and work through issues. It seems to be more like a *fire, ready, aim* approach. As I watched them struggle through meetings of all types with no process, I asked them why they didn't use process. In 100 percent of the cases, they told me they didn't know what I meant by process. I then asked a number of them how many college degrees they had. That varied, but most of them had two or three. My next question was "Did you ever learn problem-solving techniques or ways to dialogue with colleagues?" Once again, the answers were 100 percent "No!" I thought of my own answer to the last question. It too was "No!" I then decided to spend time learning about process tools for problem solving. Over the last 10 years I have had to travel down the road of business and industry to learn, but I have had some wonderful learning experiences. I have taken what I have learned and retooled the ideas for educators. The process techniques in this section have been used by businesses for many years. Most educators are not trained in process, so we end up like the system in the story—working harder versus smarter. I have used all of the ideas in this chapter many times and had great success. I hope you will have the same experience.

Did You Know

- 50 percent of problem solving should be spent analyzing facts and defining the problem.
- There is a difference between an assumption and a fact.
- Using data to make decisions and guide your thinking is optimal.

- Understanding a problem requires patience and determination.
- Members must agree on the problem and be willing to work on it.
- Teams that proceed without thinking ahead may be headed for disaster.
- When solving problems, it's important to encourage equal participation.

#89. It's a Force Field

The team sets a goal. It might be to become a professional learning community or to use the nine instructional strategies from Robert Marzano's (2001) *Classroom Instruction That Works.* It might be to design two interdisciplinary units for the upcoming year or to work with a partner to coach each other twice a month. The goal should be written at the top of a sheet of chart paper labeled Goal. Next, divide the chart paper into two columns. Title one column Driving Forces and the other column Restraining Forces. Explain that driving forces are the things that are already happening or are in place that move the team toward its goal. Restraining forces are the barriers that are keeping the team from achieving the goal. Ask the team members to brainstorm items that should be listed in the columns. When all the driving and restraining forces have been listed, have the team members look at the driving forces and decide if they have enough going for them to attempt the goal. The number of driving forces isn't important; the quality of the driving force is what's important. Then consider the restraining forces. Look at each one and say, "Does this team have the power to do something about this barrier?" If the answer is "Yes," put a star next to it. If the answer is "No, the team can't do anything about the barrier," cross it out. This is a very important step, because the team should focus only on the things it has the power to change. For example, if a barrier involves budgeting issues and the team has no control over the budget, then the team shouldn't waste energy on the barrier. After the team identifies

FORCE FIELD ANALYSIS

Driving Forces (Facilitators)	Restraining Forces (Blockers)

barriers it has the power to change, it should divide into pairs. Each pair takes a number of barriers and lists two or three solutions. The team then meets again as a whole group so that each pair can share its solutions with other team members. The team members listen to each solution and rate it as follows:

I = impossible

M = maybe, if we do a little tweaking to it

O = outstanding—let's do it

Once all the solutions have been rated, the team develops an action plan for implementing the solutions.

Materials You Will Need

the force field chart

a colored marker

#90. Let's Map It Out

The following process, which uses maps to solve problems, can be implemented in two ways. One option is to first ask team members to work individually to create maps using the model shown below and then transfer their work to a team map. A second option is to engage the entire team in working as a group to create one team map. The team decides which option will yield the best results.

If team members are going to first create individual maps, each person receives a copy of the Map organizer as shown below. In the square box, write the problem, topic, or issue. Each team member then writes key words on the five branches about the problem or topic. The five branches are as follows:

1. *History*—History means the experience team members have had with the problem, solution, or issue. This might include courses they have taken, experiences they have had, solutions they have tried, or information they have

read. The purpose is not to see who knows the most but to give team members an opportunity to reflect and see what the team knows collectively.

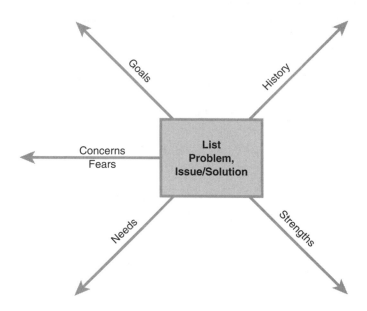

2. *Strengths*—Strengths should include individual strong points team members have in relation to the problem/ issue or solution. This information helps build the team's awareness of potential resources for solving the problem.

3. *Concerns/Fears*—What factors worry team members, or what are they afraid might or might not happen as a result of the problem/issue or solution? Acknowledging the emotional impact will help team members solve a problem.

4. *Needs*—What does a team member need in order to be willing to deal with the problem/issue or solution?

5. *Goals*—What do the team members hope will be the end result of the process?

Team members are given about five minutes to reflect and jot down their thoughts below the five different branches. When time is up, the recorder draws a large replica of the map on chart paper. Each person is assigned a color. (One person is red, another is green, and so on.) Starting with History, the recorder uses the color assigned to a person to record what he or she says. One branch is completed by all the team members before going to the next branch. Once the map has been completed, the team has a powerful visual record of what people know, feel, need, and want in connection with the problem, issue, or solution. The next step is for the team members to first look at the Goals branch and identify the common goals in regard to the problem, issue, or solution. Once this is done, they look at the Concerns/Fears and brainstorm solutions for overcoming the Concerns/Fears and accomplishing the Goal(s). When designing solutions, team members should look at the Strengths and use the individual team member strengths when possible. They should also look at Needs and work to design solutions that meet the needs of the team members, if possible. By meeting the needs of the team, the implementation will go more smoothly. As the team designs solutions, it must continuously look at the goal(s) it wants to accomplish and ask, "Does this solution move us toward our goal(s)?" If not, then the solution should be discarded. The last step in this process is to develop an action plan.

Materials You Will Need

chart paper

colored markers

individual worksheets with maps on them

#91. Let's Have a Discussion

When team members have a problem, issue, or solution they want to discuss, providing a structured format for the discussion ensures that everyone gets an opportunity to talk, emotions are expressed, and good decisions are made. Begin by having group members sit in an arrangement that allows everyone to be seen. The chart following lays out steps for a successful group discussion. The team leader takes the group through one step at a time, allowing each person a maximum of one minute for each step.

1. OBJECTIVE LEVEL

> 1. What is seen, heard, touched, smelled, and
> tasted.
> > *"The facts, ma'am, nothing but the facts."*

2. REFLECTIVE LEVEL

> 2. What is felt—emotions, moods, surprise,
> anger, joy, excitement.
> > *"How are you feeling today?"*

3. INTERPRETIVE LEVEL

> 3. Meanings, significance, purpose, and understanding.
> > *What's it all about, Alfie?"*

4. DECISION LEVEL

> 4. What will be done—actions decided, resolutions made, and next steps
> to be taken
> > *"What's it mean in the real world?"*

Objective Level—Team members state what they know about the problem, issue, or solution that is a *fact*. If someone says, "Everyone likes the solution," the team should question whether that is a fact or an assumption. If data have been collected that indicate people like the solution, then it is a fact. If there are no data and people are just making random statements about what people like, then it's an assumption. The recorder writes it down in a column under the heading "Assumptions." The team members decide whether or not they need this information to make an informed decision. If they need the information, they decide how they will collect data to find out if it is a fact. Once all of the facts have been recorded, the team moves on to the next level.

Reflective Level—Team members look at the facts and express how they feel emotionally. For example, someone might say, "I'm feeling excited about the solution because I think we need a change and this will benefit the students." Due to the personal nature of what people are sharing, this discussion is not recorded. However, the discussion helps team members know and understand the feelings of others. Once everyone has shared, move on to the next level.

Interpretive Level—Team members share any connections they have with the problem, issue, or solution. For example, someone might say, "One of the reasons I said I was excited is that I worked in another system where we implemented this and it made a major difference in student achievement. It wasn't easy, so when we get to the implementation stage, I would exercise caution because . . . " Once everyone has shared, move on to the next level.

Decision Level—The team leader says, "We have discussed the facts, we know how each person feels emotionally, and we understand the connections and experiences we each bring to the table. It is time to decide the next steps we want to take." The leader gives each team member a Post-it note to write down a suggestion for the next steps. One by one, the team members present the Post-it notes with an explanation and then place the notes in the middle of the table. After everyone has had a turn, the group prioritizes the suggestions agreed on and develops an action plan.

Materials You Will Need

> chart paper
>
> colored markers

#92. Going Fishing

This is a tool for using a structured format to identify and organize the possible causes of a problem. Draw the upper fish bone diagram as shown below. Write the problem, topic, or issue in the box on the right side of the diagram. Make sure everyone agrees on the statement that is going inside the box. Draw a long center arrow from the box and draw four to six category arrows from the centerline. Notice that all of the category arrows point to the thick centerline. Brainstorm with the team

Fishbone Diagram

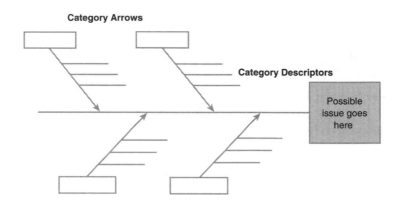

Fishbone Diagram Example

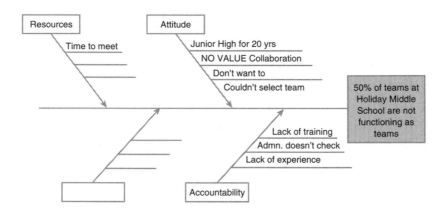

members the different categories they think might be causing the problem. After writing a category in a box, they should add key words that describe or relate to the category. A completed sample is also shown below. When the team has completed the diagram, assign the categories to different team members. Team members are to collect data to determine whether or not the category is, in fact, a cause of the problem. Set a date for the next meeting, during which team members will bring their data and determine which of the categories are actually the root causes. Once the causes have been identified, the team can discuss solutions to the causes and develop an action plan.

Materials You Will Need

chart paper

colored markers

fish bone diagram

#93. A Comprehensive Action Plan

When a more detailed action plan is required, use the planning guide shown below. Completing this action plan engages the group in a thorough discussion and helps the team identify details likely to be missed when creating simpler plans. Call the team members together and have them fill out the columns for each solution. Complete the Steps to Implement column by breaking down the tasks into multiple, detailed steps. Providing greater detail ensures that team members are clear about what must be done. The Assessment column describes how the success of the solution will be measured. Encourage the team to identify benchmarks that will challenge people to increase their professional competence, rather than establishing lower performance levels. When the action plan is completed, request that group members bring a copy of it to their team meetings every month to review their progress toward the goals. Making adjustments to the action plan as needed throughout the school year engages the team members in continuous improvement.

Completed Action Plan

Solution 1	Steps to Implement	Date to begin	Date to complete	Persons Responsible	Assessment
Attend two days of training on Instructional Strategies	1. Look at the research from Robert Marzano to see what strategies really impact student achievement	May 1, 2006	August 2006	Planning Team	100% of teachers attend the two-day training. An evaluative report from the consultant gives positive feedback of teacher attitudes, teacher involvement in the training, and teachers making connections when asked to reflect in a journal. A follow-up plan is designed by each grade level and carried out that holds the teachers accountable for using the strategies on a daily basis and the administration accountable for walk-through identifying the use of strategies. Teachers are using the strategies as evidenced in their lesson plans.
	2. Make a list of questions to ask the consultants when we call them.				
	3. Call consultant references.				
	4. Select consultant				
	5. Set up dates for training.				
	6. Notify teachers				
	7. Plan a follow-up meeting to see what next steps are once the training has been completed.				

For the Committed: Oops!

Going far beyond the call of duty, doing more than others
expect, is what excellence is all about. And it comes from
striving, maintaining the highest standards, going the extra
mile. Excellence means doing your very best. In everything. In every way.

—Anonymous

Background

One of the major reasons people don't use process tools is
that they're afraid they won't do it right and will look foolish.
I understand this because I too have had that fear. Let me
share a story that will help you see it's okay to make a mistake
in process, and that in most cases, people won't even notice.
About eight years ago, my friend Margaret Hable called me
and said, "Carol, you know how we're always trying to get
people to set goals or to describe what they really want?" I
said, "Yes! Don't tell me you've figured out an easy way to do
that." She said, "I'm not sure it's easy, but I will tell you it's
doable." Margaret proceeded to teach it to me over the phone.
It took her about an hour. I got off the phone, reviewed it,
rewrote it, practiced it, and felt ready to try this wonderful
process. It wasn't long before I had an opportunity to put it
into practice. I received a call from a high school in Chicago
that wanted to set clear goals for the next few years. I was so
excited because I knew this one was going to be a success. As
an aside, let me tell you that the little voice in the back of my
head told me to call Margaret *just* to be sure I had all the steps
down correctly. Well, I talked myself out of it. I mean, after all,
I had spent about two or more hours learning and practicing.

The day arrived. I had lots and lots of index cards ready to
get the teams to write one idea per card that we would categorize and use to design goals. I divided the staff into teams, gave
them the assignment, and off they went. I was overwhelmed at
the response to the task. I had brought 200 cards just to be safe.

The next thing I knew, all the cards were gone. I had to borrow more. It was at this point that I knew something was wrong. I couldn't remember Margaret ever mentioning that she and her team had to categorize more than 200 cards. I ran back to my directions. Next to the step for categorizing it said, "Take the 50 or so cards and with a team spend 15 minutes categorizing them" Oops! I had made a *big* mistake. How do you categorize 250 cards in 15 minutes? I almost fainted! I didn't tell anyone. I went into the bathroom by myself and screamed. I felt better! I took a big breath and went back out. I made up the rest of the process. It wasn't pretty, *but* the end result was great. The goals were so well done that when it was over, *no one* remembered the messy categorization. All they focused on were the goals. The first thing I did when I got home was call Margaret to find out how many index cards each table team was to receive and a little more about the categorization process.

I'm so glad this happened to me, although at the time I wouldn't have said that. It has helped me to relate to people when they tell me they're afraid to try. As a result of my experience, I have added a piece into my training of process called "What If." It really helps people see that it's okay to make a mistake, and if you get past the panic, you can figure out something to do to save the process. Even if it's just to say, "Oops, that didn't work. Let's try it a different way."

Did You Know

- Teams that proceed with improvements without thinking ahead may be headed toward disaster.
- Change is productive when it involves more effective ways of operating and leads to consistently improved outcomes.
- Look for win-win solutions to problems.
- When selecting a process tool, be clear about the team's purpose.
- Planning provides a road map that gives the team a sense of direction and helps ensure that key tasks aren't missed.
- Begin with the end in mind.
- Nearly every day we face possibilities and problems that affect our personal and professional lives.

- The ability not only to cope with but also to identify key issues, access information, and effectively work our way through these situations contributes to success in whatever we pursue.

#94. What's Your Concern?

The team recorder copies the diagram shown below on a large sheet of paper. The team leader states the problem/issue/ solution the team has identified. In the circle labeled Concerns, the team recorder records all the concerns the team has. All concerns are considered valid. When that circle is complete, the team members look at each concern and ask, "Does this team have the power to influence this concern in any way?" If the answer is yes, the recorder records that concern in the circle of Influence.

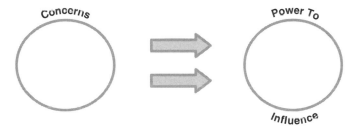

Words of caution. Often team members want to start trying to come up with solutions to validate that they have some influence. Remind the team that now is not the time for solutions but for making decisions as to whether or not the team can influence this concern. When the concerns that the team can influence have been moved to the circle of Influence, the leader tells the group that under no circumstances will they spend time talking about or telling war stories about the concerns over which they have no influence. Proactive teams focus on the problems, issues, or solutions they can change and leave the rest alone. Once the Influence circle has been completed, the team looks at the information and decides if any of the concerns can be grouped together. If so, group them. The team then develops solution criteria (see Activity #95). Divide the concerns among the team members and give them time to come up with solutions that meet the established criteria. At the next team meeting, the solutions are reported to the team members, who use the ranking below:

O = outstanding

M = maybe, with a few changes

I = impossible

When all the solutions have been presented, the team members select the ones they are going to try. The action plan chart shown below may be used to plan for each solution.

Materials You Will Need

colored markers

chart paper

Action Plan				
Concern 1	Steps to Implement	Date	Persons Involved	Assessment
Solutions 1 _____ 2 _____				
Concern 2				
Solutions 1 _____ 2 _____				

#95. King or Queen for a Day

This is a good process activity for a team that is helping one person solve a problem. It is called King or Queen for a Day because the attention is totally focused on the person who wants help from the team. The team leader or facilitator leads this process.

The first step is to ask the person who is the king or queen to spend three minutes giving a history of the problem. The king or queen explains who, what, where, when, actions taken, and anything that will help the team to understand the problem. The team members must remain at a zero voice level. They may not ask questions or talk among themselves, although they may jot down questions as the king or queen is talking.

Next, allow the team members to ask *clarifying questions.* They should not ask about possible solutions. For example, "Have you tried giving feedback to this person?" is a solution question, not a clarifying question. Clarifying questions are usually about something the king or queen has said. Some examples of clarifying questions are as follows: "Let me make sure I understand what you said . . . Can you give me some more information about that? Or when you said . . . what did you mean?" Team members should also avoid telling war stories about their experiences with a similar problem and how they solved it. Remember, the focus is on the king or queen. This step takes about five minutes.

The king or queen is asked to give some criteria that a solution would have to meet in order for it to be acceptable for trial. Examples are as follows: (a) it has to be a solution that doesn't take three months to implement, or (b) it can't cost any money, or (c) both parties have to save face.

While it may be challenging to think about these criteria at this time, the team members can work more efficiently and smoothly if they know in advance what the criteria are. This prevents team members from feeling like they have wasted their time coming up with solutions that are unacceptable to the king or queen. This step takes about a minute or two.

The king or queen leaves the group for 5 or 10 minutes. At this time, the team members individually reflect on solutions. Each member writes one solution per Post-it note. If a person has five solutions, they will use five Post-it notes. There is no talking among the team members because it decreases the number of solutions generated.

The king or queen returns. Each team member presents his or her solutions to the king or queen. A team member reads one solution at a time, *then* hands the king or queen the Post-it note with the solution. The king or queen rates the solution one of the following ways:

O = outstanding; I'll do it

M = if we can do a little adjustment, I can use it

I = impossible because . . .

If a team member has the same or a similar solution that another team member is sharing, he or she should give it to the king or queen at the same time to avoid repetition. If any of the solutions are labeled "M," the entire team can join in the discussion of how to adjust.

The king or queen reviews all the solutions that were marked "O," then develops an action plan. See Activity #94.

The team sets up a meeting with the king or queen two weeks from the date of this meeting to see how things are going.

#96. What Hat Are You Wearing?

There are times during the problem-solving process when a high-level discussion is appropriate. This could be a discussion of the problem, of an issue, of the solution, or a discussion about how people are feeling. Using a specific process for dialogue helps ensure that such discussions are as effective as possible. Dr. Edward de Bono developed a thinking process called the Six Hats. What Hat Are You Wearing? is a modification of this process that allows for creative problem solving by avoiding negativity and group arguments.

Create a large chart with six hats colored as indicated below. Share the definitions of the hats with the team. Pose the problem, issue, or solution the team is dealing with and ask the team to "put on" one of the hats for a period of time. Alternatives to this are to assign each team member a different hat to "wear" for a period of time, or to ask the team members to select a hat to wear and discuss the problem, issue, or solution from that perspective. Another alternative is to have team members wear a hat they don't normally wear.

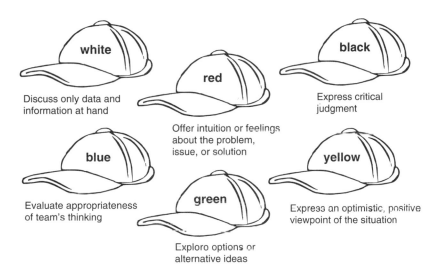

white
Discuss only data and information at hand

red
Offer intuition or feelings about the problem, issue, or solution

black
Express critical judgment

blue
Evaluate appropriateness of team's thinking

green
Explore options or alternative ideas

yellow
Express an optimistic, positive viewpoint of the situation

Materials You Will Need

Different Hats chart

#97. The Big 10

Due to the commitment of time and energy required for this problem-solving process, it is best used when trying to solve a major problem, deal with a highly charged issue, or implement a complex solution. Examples are a team that wants to learn about and implement differentiated instruction or a school that is trying to implement a professional learning community. The Big 10 is an excellent process because it involves the people who are facing the problem or are going to implement the solution from the start. The buy-in is very high with this process.

Step 1: Education

This step is designed to increase the group members' knowledge so that they are able to make good decisions about the problem, issue, or solution to be implemented. The purpose is to raise everyone's awareness level of both factual and erroneous information. There are many ways to achieve this step. The team could watch a video on the problem, the issue, or the solution. Team members could read articles, go to a conference, listen to a guest speaker, or visit a site that is facing the same problem/issue or solution. This step could take one hour, a week, or a month, depending on the level of knowledge needed, so that the team can have informed discussions and successfully implement solutions.

Step 2: Pay Value Chart

Once the team members have sufficient understanding of the issue, they are ready to talk about the value to each team member of a successful solution. This important step helps motivate team members. *Pay value* refers to "What's in it for me?" If team members believe they will benefit from the solution, they will be more likely to embrace it. Draw a Pay Value chart similar to the one shown below and have teams follow the directions on the chart. The categories on the chart should correspond to the people who will be affected by the *solution or the change.* If the group is large, divide team members into groups of five and have each group complete the chart. It will be easier to collect the data from 5 to 10 charts than from 50 to 120 individual people.

1. Sit at tables in groups of four or five team members.

2. Have them discuss the benefits of solving the problem, dealing with the issue, or successfully implementing the solution. List the benefits for each stakeholder group in the appropriate column.

3. Collect the charts, compile the data, and share the results with the entire team.

4. Use the data to determine if the team is ready to go on to the next step. If the chart has a lot of columns that have nothing in them, then the team members are not seeing the value of dealing with the problem, issue, or solution. The team would then go back to Step 1 and continue with education.

Teachers	Support Staff	Administrators	Students	Parents	Community

Step 3: Voice Chart

The team has had an opportunity to learn about the problem or issue and determine the benefits of implementing a solution. Now is the time to give team members an opportunity to use a voice chart to express their concerns and needs in a public forum. This will help prevent team members from going underground with their concerns and possibly sabotaging the implementation plan. Once again, if the team is large, divide it into groups of five. Draw the chart below and follow the directions on the chart.

Discuss the questions below and write the responses in the appropriate columns.

- What do you need to do so you can support the change or the solution or solve the problem?
- What do you need from your administrators so you will support the change or the solution?

1. YOU	2. ADMINISTRATION	3. CENTRAL OFFICE

- What do you need from the central office so that you will support the change or the solution?

Collect the completed charts, collate the data, and share them with the team. At this time, have the administration tell team members which of their needs they can support and which they cannot. Have someone from the central office come to the meeting and do the same. It is very important to follow through on this step. Otherwise, credibility will be lost and there is a good chance that the solution will fail. This part of the process will also help the team members become aware of steps and resources they need to put into the action plan.

Step 4: Values Vote

This is a step that many teams leave out. However, people act according to their values. Values influence choices and are the sustaining source for perseverance when things get tough. Turn to Activity #21 to learn a process for determining values. Once the team members take the values vote, they look at the common values and determine if the change or the solution is supported by what they value. For example, if the vote shows that working collaboratively is a common value and the team is trying to design a professional learning community, there is a higher likelihood of success than if the vote indicated that few people valued collaboration.

Step 5: Mission

Help team members understand that this is not the same as the mission of the school. Instead, it refers to the team's mission regarding the problem, issue, or solution it has to implement. Let's go back to the example of the team designing a professional learning community. That team would define what its mission was in regard to professional learning communities. The mission might sound like "Our mission is to work together to design a plan to implement professional learning communities as the model for our middle school teams." It might seem unnecessary for a team to define its mission in such specific terms, but oftentimes team members are confused as to their purpose. If asked why they are meeting, members will say things like "I don't know for sure" or "The principal said we would be meeting once a month to do something." It's hard to get team members to function at a high level when they don't clearly understand what they are supposed to accomplish.

Step 6: The Big Picture

This engaging and exciting step occurs when the team has a high level of buy-in and is ready to envision what the desired outcome will look and sound like. The team leader clearly states the solution that has been agreed upon. The leader writes the statement, "In a year, if we are [write in the solution] at the highest level, what will we see and hear happening in our school?" Each team member is given a pack of Post-it notes, and they list each descriptor they generate on a Post-it note. If a team member has five descriptors, then he or she will have five Post-it notes.

Allow team members 10 to 15 minutes. Then have individuals share the ideas on the Post-it notes. While sharing, they put the notes on chart paper and begin to categorize. Duplicates are placed on top of each other, and the sharing continues. Once this is done, the team members reflect on the categories and decide which ones create a clear picture of what the end result will look and sound like. They determine if anything has been left out. The team now has a clear picture of what the solution

The Big Picture

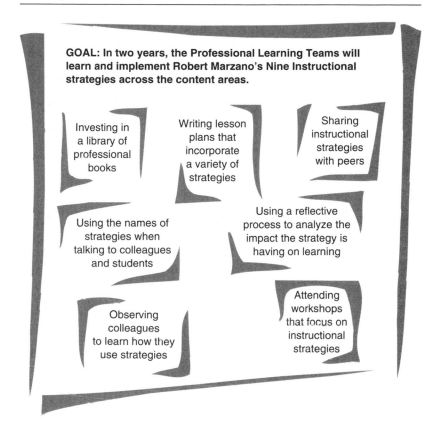

GOAL: In two years, the Professional Learning Teams will learn and implement Robert Marzano's Nine Instructional strategies across the content areas.

Investing in a library of professional books

Writing lesson plans that incorporate a variety of strategies

Sharing instructional strategies with peers

Using the names of strategies when talking to colleagues and students

Using a reflective process to analyze the impact the strategy is having on learning

Observing colleagues to learn how they use strategies

Attending workshops that focus on instructional strategies

will look like and sound like when it has been successfully implemented. Using this picture, the team begins to plan with the end in mind. This picture is also helpful in making decisions as the plan unfolds. If a team member suggests an idea, it should be measured by how it would impact the end result. If the new idea doesn't lead to the desired result, the team does not spend any time on it. If the idea does lead to the desired result, then the team considers it.

Step 7: Force Field Analysis

Once the team members have determined the desired result, they can use a force field analysis process. Activity #89 gives directions for the force field analysis. This process helps team members determine what is already in place that will help them solve the problem, deal with the issue, or implement the solution. Even more important, it helps the team members to know what is in place that will keep them from being successful. The team then identifies actions that would strengthen the driving forces and would remove or weaken the restraining forces. These actions become part of the implementation plan.

Step 8: Solution Criteria/Solutions

Once the driving and restraining forces have been identified, it is time to design actions or solutions for them. Before the team divides up to do this, the members identify criteria that the solutions must meet in order for the team to implement them. This prevents the discouragement that occurs when team members spend valuable time generating solutions and are then told they can't be implemented because, for example, they cost too much or take too much time or won't be supported by the central office. Identifying solution criteria eliminates this problem. Here are some examples of solution criteria:

✓ A critical mass accepts the solution

✓ The solution moves us toward the end result we created

✓ It is within the budget constraints

✓ It can be implemented in a reasonable amount of time

✓ It is safe

✓ It benefits students

Once the solution criteria have been discussed and agreed upon, the team members work in pairs to come up with solutions. When they present the solutions to the team, the team rates each solution according to the criteria. If a solution meets the criteria, it gets an *O* for outstanding. If a solution meets all but one or two of the criteria, but with a little more work it would be a good one, it gets an *M* for maybe. If a solution is presented and it doesn't meet the criteria, then it gets an *I* for impossible. When all the solutions have been rated, the entire team works on the M's and adds them to the O's.

Step 9: Developing the Action Plan

Once the solutions have been agreed upon, it's time to develop a plan for implementing. The grid below is an example of an action plan sheet.

Turn to Activities #93 and #94 for two more examples of action plans.

Solution	Step & Desired Outcome	Who	Dates Begin/End	Resources	Assessment	Comments

Step 10: Celebrate

Celebration is a very important part of the problem-solving process. Celebrating accomplishments leads to high team morale and creates energy for the project. Chapter 10 has many suggestions for celebrations. The key is to be sure the team holds itself to high standards.

The entire 10-step process takes a significant time commitment, which is why this process is not appropriate for every team task. The team members determine the pace at which they will go through the steps. It is important to remember to do some type of assessment at the end of each step.

Materials You Will Need

Activities #21, #93, and #94

descriptions of Activities #113–#122

chart paper

colored markers

copies of any charts for the step you are on

9

Giving and Receiving Feedback

When I think of giving and receiving feedback, I often think about my first years as a teacher. Once a year, the administrator would come around and visit my class. He would take notes, smile sweetly, and leave. One time, I got a note in my mailbox that said, "See me!" It was like having a near-death experience. You know—your life passes in front of you. I found myself wondering if I had broken any school rules, reprimanded the wrong child, sneered at a colleague, or made a negative comment about my administrator. As I walked through the door of his office, using my best placating body language, I said, "You wanted to see me?" It turned out that it was conference time. Time to receive feedback on my ability to teach. It started out with a lot of "goods" and a few "greats," but as the clock ticked on, I heard the dreaded word "however." I braced myself for what I knew was coming. "Carol," he said, "you need to do better on classroom management. Also, you might want to work on . . ." The words became a blur. I felt like a failure. I didn't hear another word. I just nodded passively while he did all the talking. I remember getting up, smiling my best fake smile, and thanking him for all his help. I went back to my room and continued to teach the way I had always taught.

> *Was I uncommitted, uncaring, and insubordinate? No. I wanted to be a good teacher, but in those days, we didn't really know a lot about teaching or giving feedback. I am proud to say that great strides have been made in my profession in regard to giving and receiving feedback. As a result, I no longer teach as I did during my first few years.*

W. Edwards Deming (2000) says that organizations should institute on-the-job training and vigorous programs of education and self-improvement for everyone. What better way to do this than through team feedback on performance? A team should have a system that gives each team member an opportunity to reflect on himself or herself first privately and then share those reflections with the team. It should also provide feedback about whether or not the team is sticking to its mission and about how the team is abiding by its norms. This feedback should be given daily, monthly, or yearly, depending on the team's needs. Every time feedback is given, an action plan should be developed that outlines what the team needs to do to perform at a higher level. The team should strive for continued growth and development.

The outcomes of team feedback on performance should be as follows:

1. Creating and managing trust

2. Facilitating learning

3. Developing autonomy

Each of these goals is explained as follows:

1. *Creating and managing trust:* Trust must be established before true feedback can be given or received. If trust has not been established, the team members will "nice" each other to death: they will not tell the truth, and they will make excuses for why someone may have acted a certain way or why a task did not get done. The team must work hard to move beyond this stage in order for real growth to occur. Trust is a complex

concept: it is being able to rely on the team. It is believing that team members have your best interest at heart and that their words and opinions are reliable. It is believing the team will act in a fair way when it comes to feedback. It is knowing the team has integrity.

2. *Facilitating learning*: As a result of the feedback process, team members should learn something about themselves, about each other, and about the team as a whole. The process should be one that gives the members hope that they can get better through professional growth and development. They should find themselves thinking differently than they did when they first started together.

3. *Developing autonomy*: A team that has reached this level is one that does not need much help from the outside. It has reached a high level of self-awareness, self-evaluation, and self-modifiability. Members of such a team are aware of their behaviors and the impact of the behaviors on fellow team members. They can analyze, evaluate, and modify their team behaviors as well as design their own prescriptions for growth. They are in a continuous state of growth and are excited about where they are going.

This chapter is important because it is through feedback on performance that the team is able to reach the performing stage. The ideas in this chapter are best carried out by an assigned observer on the team.

SIMPLE THINGS TO DO: I REALLY DON'T WANT TO KNOW

A smile in giving honest criticism can make the difference between resentment and reform.

—Phillip Steinmetz

Background

I have no idea if the story you are about to read is true. I believe it is, because I can't imagine a teacher telling it about herself just to be funny. The story goes like this.

One day a teacher was teaching a lesson. As she turned from the board, she noticed a young man with his hand in the air. She called on him. He said, "Mrs. Lee, do you like what you do?" "Yes, I like what I do!" said Mrs. Lee, and went on teaching. About halfway through the lesson, the young man raised his hand again. "Yes, son, what is it?" said Mrs. Lee. "Are you sure you like what you do?" asked the young man. Mrs. Lee responded, "I told you, yes; now don't interrupt the lesson again." "Are you sure?" said the young man. The teacher placed her hands on her hips and with a stern look said, "For the last time, *yes*, I like what I do." The young man looked sheepishly at the teacher and said, "Then why don't you tell your face?" The teacher told me that in all her years of teaching, she had never received feedback that affected her so profoundly.

Did You Know

- An individual can increase learning tremendously when he or she receives feedback.
- All human beings have blind spots that can limit their potential.
- The most helpful kind of feedback is very specific.
- Comments must be honest, but the dignity of the individual receiving them should have top consideration.

#98. Reflective Questions

The first step in this activity is for you to decide if you want the team to receive and give feedback concerning one of the following areas:

- Team roles
- Individual performance as a team member
- The team's functioning as a whole

Once you choose the area, look at the questions below and rewrite them accordingly.

- What was it you expected to do?
- What do you think you did well?
- What would you do differently?
- What support do you need from the team?

For example, if the team is going to discuss team roles or team member behavior, the questions can stay as is, but if the team is going to discuss the team as a whole, you need to reword the questions as follows:

- What were we expected to do?
- What have we done well?
- What should we do differently?
- What support do we need to continue or change our performance?

Write the questions on a chart and hang them on a wall. Tell the members which of the three areas they are going to focus on for the meeting. Give the members 10 minutes of silence to think of their responses. Once the time limit is up, take one question at a time and ask each team member to respond. Record the responses. Summarize the responses for each question and thank team members for being open and honest. Remind them how important feedback is to the growth of the team.

Materials You Will Need

1 copy of the questions listed in the activity

a piece of chart paper

masking tape

#99. PCI

Place the following chart on the wall.

P	C	I

Lead the team members in a discussion about what they have accomplished as a team that is positive, what they have concerns about, and what has happened or not happened that is interesting. The recorder records the responses under the appropriate column.

You can use this chart as an individual feedback tool. The observer asks each individual to fill out a copy of the PCI chart. Members are to reflect on what they think they have done for the team that is *positive*, what about their individual performance is a *concern*, and what they have found *interesting* about themselves as they have worked on becoming a team member. Each team member shares his or her responses with the team. Again, this is a tool that is open to many creative adaptations.

Materials You Will Need

a large PCI chart

1 copy of the PCI chart per person

a colored marker

#100. Temperature Check

Place the Temperature Check chart on the wall. Tell each team member that this is a quick way to check on the team's climate. Explain each of the categories on the chart. Then model one or two responses a team member might make. For example, a team member might select the heading Appreciations and say, "I would like to tell the team members how much I appreciate the fact they allowed me to disagree with dignity." Another team member might select Puzzles and say, "I still don't understand how we're going to have time to do the project we said we were going to do. Could someone help me out in five seconds or less?" Someone else might say, "I have a complaint. We were really off task today. I'd like to offer my services in giving a high five sign when we've been on task for five minutes or more." Another member might say, "I want to share a wish. I wish we could snap our fingers and make some of the barriers we're facing go away."

When everyone has had at least one opportunity to respond, thank the team and close the meeting.

TEMPERATURE CHECK

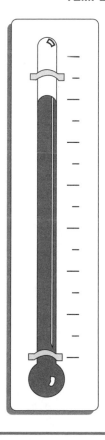

APPRECIATIONS

Something you appreciate about the group, an individual, or a group process.

COMPLAINTS

Something that bothers you. Offer an alternative.

PUZZLES

Something you are confused about.

HOPES, WISHES

Something you hope or wish for concerning the team or its mission.

Materials You Will Need

1 large Temperature Check chart

masking tape

#101. Support Me

Ask each person to think of how he or she could become a better team member. Ask everyone to set one or two goals for growth in relation to being a good team member and write these goals on the handout. In two months or so, ask the members to bring their goal sheets to the meeting. Each team member shares his or her goals with the team and asks for support. After four months, the team members revisit their goals and ask the group for feedback on how they are doing. If they need help, the group brainstorms ways to support them. For example, one team member may be quiet and want to speak up more. If this is not happening over a period of weeks, the team may think of ways to be sure the person has an opportunity to speak up.

GOALS I'VE SET FOR MYSELF

Name: _____

Goal 1

Goal 2

Materials You Will Need

goal sheets

Things That Take Effort:
The First Cut Is the Deepest

Criticism should not be querulous and wasting, but guiding, instructive, and inspiring.

—Ralph Waldo Emerson

Background

In the early 1980s I was working for a very large school district that wanted to do a massive staff development training. Since we had 3,000 teachers, we decided that we would train a team of four people at each school to deliver the training on designated staff development days. I spent months training the trainers. They were like my children. I was so proud of their hard work. One point I kept stressing was that a good trainer always asks for feedback, responds to the feedback, and makes adjustments when possible.

The day arrived for the trainers to begin training others. All of us were full of fear, excitement, and high hopes. The training ended at 3:00 p.m. At 3:15 I heard a knock on my office door. Four of my trainers were standing with feedback sheets in their hands and big tears in their eyes. "Read these, read these!" they cried. As I began reading, I couldn't understand what they could be crying about. The feedback comments were great. But as I neared the bottom of the pile, my face fell. I read the following comments:

The trainers were an insult.

Too much time on rear.

This sucks.

One of our trainers can't speak correct English.

Who's the stupid that punched the holes wrong in my handouts?

I must say I was stunned that any professional would write such unkind and unprofessional comments on a feedback sheet to his or her colleagues. I wondered what these people would do to a student who dared do the same to them. I would say they'd be in major trouble, wouldn't you?

Did You Know

- Criticism is most effective when it sounds like praise.
- It is more effective not to find fault; find a remedy.
- In order for feedback to be effective, there must be a basic trust in one another.
- Feedback should not be judgmental.
- Feedback must not be interpretative.

#102. Liked/Didn't Like

Place the following chart on the wall:

Things I Liked	Things I Didn't Like	Suggestions

Remind the team members that when they are giving this type of feedback, it is imperative to treat situations and people with dignity. The feedback must be specific and not a "shame and blame game." Each team member responds using specific examples. Under the column Things I Didn't Like, the person has to make a suggestion about how to make the situation better. For example, a team member might say, "I didn't like the fact that we were off task 20 minutes of our meeting. My suggestion is that we open our awareness level and see if this happens at our next meeting. If it does, we may want to review our roles to see who should be keeping us on task, talk about why it's not happening, and discuss how we can help this person keep us on task. Or we may discover that the person is trying to keep us on task and we're not responding. We might want to look at why and how we can prevent this from becoming a habit."

Each team member has an opportunity to respond to any of the columns. A person can pass but has to say why. The recorder records the responses.

When everyone has had a turn, the team members look at what they liked, turn to the chapter on celebrations in this book, and celebrate. They look at the things they didn't like and discuss and plan what they can do to prevent these things from happening.

Materials You Will Need

1 large Liked/Didn't Like chart

a colored marker

masking tape

#103. How Productive Were We?

Distribute copies of the How Productive Were We? feedback sheet and ask each member to fill one out. The recorder records the team responses, using a large mockup of the feedback sheet. The team then discusses areas it needs to work on.

Materials You Will Need

1 large How Productive Were We? chart and 1 copy for each team member

a colored marker

masking tape

How Productive Were We?

1. Effective Use of Time						
1	**2**	**3**	**4**	**5**	**6**	**7**
Much time spent without purpose		Got off track frequently		Did well, once we got our ideas clear		No wasted effort—stayed on target

2. Development of Ideas						
1	**2**	**3**	**4**	**5**	**6**	**7**
Little done to generate ideas		Ideas were imposed on the group by a few		Friendly session but not creative		Ideas were encouraged and fully explored

3. Ability to Decide Issues						
1	**2**	**3**	**4**	**5**	**6**	**7**
Poor resolution of differences		Let one person rule		Made compromises to get the job done		Genuine agreement and support

4. Overall Productivity						
1	**2**	**3**	**4**	**5**	**6**	**7**
Did not accomplish our goals		Barely accomplished the job		Just did what we had to		Held a highly productive session

SOURCE: Kagan, S. (1994). *Cooperative Learning*. San Clemente, CA: Kagan Cooperative Learning Company. Reprinted with permission from Kagan Publishing, Kagan, Spencer—*Cooperative Learning* 1994, Kagan Publishing, San Clemente, CA. 800-933-2667. www.KaganOnline.com.

#104. How Helpful Was I?

Distribute copies of the How Helpful Was I? sheet and ask each member to fill one out. Have the team share its responses and discuss what items it needs to work on. Have members discuss what kind of help they might get from the team, and ask for feedback from the team.

Materials You Will Need

> 1 How Helpful Was I? sheet per team member (see p. 190)

#105. It's a Reflection

Distribute copies of the Reflection sheet and ask each team member to complete one. The recorder collects the sheets and records the responses on a large mockup of the sheet. The team members discuss what they need to work on and develop an action plan.

Materials You Will Need

> 1 Reflection sheet per team member (see p. 191)
>
> 1 large mockup of Reflection sheet
>
> a colored marker
>
> masking tape

#106. How Are We Doing?

The How Are We Doing? feedback sheet should be completed after the team has met four or five times. Distribute the sheet and ask the team members to reflect on the team over the past few meetings. Once team members have completed the sheets, the team recorder tallies the responses and gives the team feedback. Lead members in a discussion about what they have learned about themselves and the team. Then have them discuss what they need to work on and what they will do to improve.

Materials You Will Need

> 1 How Are We Doing? sheet per team member (see p. 192)

How Helpful Was I?

1. When I knew an answer or had an idea, I shared it.

2. I encouraged others in my group.

3. I used names.

4. I felt encouraged by people in my group.

5. When my answer was not the same as my partner's, I tried to find out why.

6. When I did not understand something, I asked my teammates.

7. When my teammates did not understand, I helped them.

Goal Setting

What can you do to make your group better?

SOURCE: Kagan, S. (1994). *Cooperative Learning*. San Clemente, CA: Kagan Cooperative Learning Company. Reprinted with permission from Kagan Publishing, Kagan, Spencer—*Cooperative Learning* 1994, Kagan Publishing, San Clemente, CA. 800-933-2667. www.KaganOnline.com.

Reflection

Use This Scale:

1. Strongly Agree
2. Agree
3. Somewhat Agree
4. Disagree
5. Strongly Disagree

Name _____

Team Name _____

Date _____

My Team	**Circle the Number**
(1) Had clear goals	Agree 1 2 3 4 5 Disagree
(2) Made progress toward the goals	Agree 1 2 3 4 5 Disagree
(3) Stayed on task	Agree 1 2 3 4 5 Disagree
(4) Made decisions based on views of all	Agree 1 2 3 4 5 Disagree

My Teammates	**Circle the Number**
(1) Listened well to each other	Agree 1 2 3 4 5 Disagree
(2) Helped each other by giving useful suggestions	Agree 1 2 3 4 5 Disagree
(3) Were respectful of all points of view	Agree 1 2 3 4 5 Disagree
(4) All participated	Agree 1 2 3 4 5 Disagree

My suggestions for improvement:

SOURCE: Kagan, S. (1994). *Cooperative Learning.* San Clemente, CA: Kagan Cooperative Learning Company. Reprinted with permission from Kagan Publishing, Kagan, Spencer—*Cooperative Learning* 1994, Kagan Publishing, San Clemente, CA. 800-933-2667. www.KaganOnline.com.

How Are We Doing?

---

1. What one word would you use to describe how the team was today?

2. What one word would describe the way you would like the team to be?

3. Is everyone participating?
Yes, always____ Usually____ Occasionally____ Rarely____ No, never____
If not, why not? _____

4. Are you (everyone on team) trying to make each other feel good?
Yes, always____ Usually____ Occasionally____ Rarely____ No, never____

5. Are you trying to help each other feel able to talk and say what you think?
Yes, always____ Usually____ Occasionally____ Rarely____ No, never____

6. Are you listening to each other?
Yes, always____ Usually____ Occasionally____ Rarely____ No, never____

7. Are you showing you are listening by nodding at each other?
Yes, always____ Usually____ Occasionally____ Rarely____ No, never____

8. Are you saying "That's good" to each other when you like something?
Yes, always____ Usually____ Occasionally____ Rarely____ No, never____

9. Are you asking each other questions?
Yes, always____ Usually____ Occasionally____ Rarely____ No, never____

10. Are you listening and really trying to answer these questions?
Yes, always____ Usually____ Occasionally____ Rarely____ No, never____

11. Are you paying attention to each other?
Yes, always____ Usually____ Occasionally____ Rarely____ No, never____

12. Is there any one person talking most of the time?
Yes ____ No ____

SOURCE: Kagan, S. (1994). *Cooperative Learning*. San Clemente, CA: Kagan Cooperative Learning Company. Reprinted with permission from Kagan Publishing, Kagan, Spencer—*Cooperative Learning* 1994, Kagan Publishing, San Clemente, CA. 800-933-2667.www.KaganOnline.com.

FOR THE COMMITTED:
I'M ON THE OUTSIDE LOOKING IN

No one so thoroughly appreciates the value of constructive criticism as the person who gives it.

—V. R. Benner

Background

In order for any organization or team to grow, it needs time for reflection, autonomy, and collaboration with others. Many teams find themselves in situations in which these three factors are almost impossible to attain. Coaches have known about these factors for years. What coach would not have his or her team reflect on the previous game? What coach does not reserve the right to choose what he or she thinks are the best plays for the game? What coach does not preach collaboration on the field? What coach does not give immediate feedback on performance? I suggest it would be unconscionable not to take any of these options from a coach. Why, then, do we think we can become a winning team without conducting business as coaches do?

Did You Know

- Feedback helps the learner by correcting his or her own subjective perception.
- Feedback increases awareness and understanding of the team process.
- Each of us sees the world through our own autobiography. We assume our perceptions are true. Feedback helps us see a different perspective.
- We must be aware of each team member's sensitivity level or threshold for receiving feedback.
- Feedback should not come before members have a fairly clear picture of each other.
- When giving feedback, each team member must report only for himself or herself.

#107. Portrait of Myself

Ask the team members to keep a log of their behaviors within the team, their feelings, what they think they have contributed to the team, and what they need to work on. They keep the logs for four or five meetings. Remind them to bring their logs to the sixth meeting, which will be devoted to the sharing of the reflections. Each team member reflects on one issue at a time, going around the team. Each team member asks the other members for feedback on the reality of his or her perceptions.

Materials You Will Need

logs

#108. It's Conference Time

Ask all team members to select a partner to be their coach. Have team members tell their coaches what behaviors to observe over a two- to four-week period. They decide together how the coach will collect the data. Once the data are collected, the partners are to have a conference. Ask the coaches to talk as little as possible and let their partners talk, because the person who talks the most learns the most. The coach may want to refer to Activity #71 and use the self-assessment questions.

Materials You Will Need

whatever is necessary to collect data

#109. Let's Get Social

Have the team observer collect data using the sociogram sheet in this activity. The directions are on the sheet. The observer does not participate in the team meeting when he or she is collecting the data. Ask the observer not to share the information with the team. Two weeks later, ask the observer to do another sociogram. After the second sociogram, have the observer share the data from both sociograms with the team. Have the team members discuss any patterns they see: who participated the most, who participated the least, and any other relevant information they can glean from the data. They then make recommendations that will help the team achieve equity in participation levels.

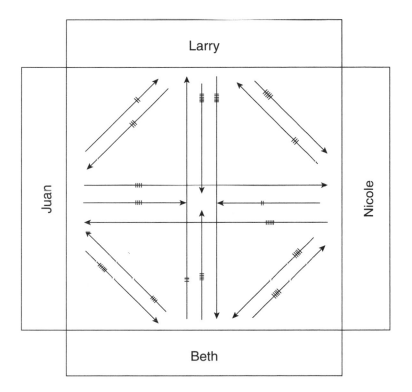

Materials You Will Need

2 sociogram sheets

THE SOCIOGRAM

Instructions: The figure below represents a table. Enter the names of team members along the sides of the square, corresponding to where they sit during the meeting. When someone speaks, draw an arrow from the speaker to the person addressed by the remark. Use a slash mark across that arrow each time the pattern is repeated. If the recipient answers the remark, draw a separate arrow from this person (who is now the speaker) to the first person (who is now being addressed). If a remark is to no one in particular, draw the arrow from the speaker to the center of the square.

#110. Hopes and Concerns

Give team members copies of the Hopes and Concerns sheet during the first team meeting. Tell them to complete the sheets over the next two weeks and to bring the completed sheets to the following meeting. In that meeting, lead the team members in a discussion about how they are doing in light of what they wrote on their sheets.

HOPES AND CONCERNS

Instructions: Jot down your hopes and concerns for this project. You will probably be asked to share your answers with your teammates.

- What are your hopes for this project?
- What do you personally want to achieve or experience?
- What do you hope the team accomplishes?
- What are your concerns about this project?
- What are your concerns about this team?

© 2006 Oriel Incorporated. All Rights Reserved.

Materials You Will Need

1 Hopes and Concerns sheet per team member

#111. Did I Help?

Give each team member three Did I Help? sheets and ask them to complete one after each team meeting for three weeks. At the end of three weeks, all team members evaluate their performance and share their responses with the team. The team can give additional feedback to the individual team members.

Materials You Will Need

3 copies of the Did I Help? sheet per team member

Did I Help?

Name _____   Group Name _____

Date _____

	Often	Sometimes	Never
1. I checked to make sure everyone understood what I did.			
2. I answered any questions that were asked.			
3. I gave explanations whenever I could.			
4. I asked specific questions about what I didn't understand.			
5. When I had difficulty, I got extra practice or help.			
6. I paraphrased what others said to be sure I understood.			

How can I be more helpful?

SOURCE: Kagan, S. (1994). *Cooperative Learning*. San Clemente, CA: Kagan Cooperative Learning Company. Reprinted with permission from Kagan Publishing, Kagan, Spencer—*Cooperative Learning* 1994, Kagan Publishing, San Clemente, CA. 800-933-2667. www.KaganOnline.com.

#112. Recipe for a Successful Team

Every three months, distribute the feedback sheet called Recipe for a Successful Team. Ask the team members to complete the sheet and bring it to the next team meeting. Devote the entire team meeting to discussing the results. Have the recorder record the results. Let the team decide if it needs additional training, a change of roles, outside support, and so on.

Materials You Will Need

1 Recipe for a Successful Team sheet per team member

Recipe for a Successful Team

Instructions: Read the statements and circle a number to indicate how well each describes your team. Be sure to complete all pages.

	Strongly Agree			Strongly Disagree
1. We agree on our mission.	1	2	3	4
2. We see the mission as workable.	1	2	3	4
3. We have a clear vision and can progress steadily toward our goals.	1	2	3	4
4. We are clear about project goals.	1	2	3	4
5. We are clear about the purpose of individual steps, meetings, discussions, and decisions.	1	2	3	4
6. We have an improvement plan.	1	2	3	4
7. We have a flowchart describing the project steps.	1	2	3	4
8. We refer to our planning documents when discussing what direction to take next.	1	2	3	4
9. We know what resources and training are needed throughout our project.	1	2	3	4
10. We have formally assigned roles.	1	2	3	4
11. We understand which roles belong to one person and which are shared, and how shared roles are switched.	1	2	3	4
12. We use each member's and involve everyone in team activities.	1	2	3	4
13. Team members speak with clarity and directness.	1	2	3	4
14. Team members listen actively.	1	2	3	4
15. Team members avoid interrupting and talking when others are speaking.	1	2	3	4

	Strongly Agree			Strongly Disagree
16. Each team member initiates discussion.	1	2	3	4
17. Each team member seeks information and opinions.	1	2	3	4
18. Each team member suggests procedures for reaching goals.	1	2	3	4
19. Each team member clarifies, summarizes, or elaborates on ideas.	1	2	3	4
20. Each team member acts as a gatekeeper.	1	2	3	4
21. Each team member compromises and is creative in resolving differences.	1	2	3	4
22. Each team member praises and corrects others with equal fairness.	1	2	3	4
23. We discuss how decisions will be made.	1	2	3	4
24. We explore important issues by polling.	1	2	3	4
25. We decide important issues by consensus.	1	2	3	4
26. We use data as the basis for our decisions.	1	2	3	4
27. We have reasonably balanced participation.	1	2	3	4
28. We have open discussions regarding ground rules.	1	2	3	4
29. We openly state or acknowledge norms.	1	2	3	4
30. We are sensitive to nonverbal communication.	1	2	3	4
31. We comment and intervene to correct group process problems.	1	2	3	4

	Strongly Agree			Strongly Disagree
32. We contribute equally to group process and meeting content.	1	2	3	4
33. We demand to see data before making decisions and question anyone who tries to act on hunches alone.	1	2	3	4
34. We use basic statistical tools to investigate problems and to gather and analyze data.	1	2	3	4
35. We dig for root causes of problems.	1	2	3	4
36. We seek permanent solutions rather than rely on quick fixes.	1	2	3	4

10

Celebrating Successes

In April of this year I received a call from an organization that wanted me to do a motivational speech for them. They were celebrating last year's production rate. Their quality defect was zero, they had employed 25 new workers, and their next year's projections were the highest ever. The chamber of commerce had named them Outstanding Business of the Year. I told them, "No problem, I look forward to it." I marked August on my calendar and went about my business.

In early August the CEO called and said there had been a slight modification to the plan. The small celebration had turned into a major event. The entire town wanted to join in. There was going to be a parade through town with floats, costumes, the works. The parade would culminate at the high school stadium, where the mayor and others would give their speeches. I was to be the last act. I would do my motivational speech from the football field to thousands.

Believe me, I was not pleased. In fact, I was in a panic. I found it hard to believe people would enjoy a three-hour event in hundred-degree weather. I was no longer looking forward to the engagement.

The day arrived. I drove an hour and a half to this small southern town. As I drove into the parking lot, I was surprised. Not only were there floats, but there also were hot air balloons, concession stands, and thousands milling around with excited faces. As we all assembled, hundreds of balloons were sent up to the loud cheers of the public. The mayor and others spoke briefly. They finished. It was now my turn to end the celebration on a high.

I closed my eyes and saw myself as my favorite rock star, Tina Turner. I took a deep breath, shot out of my chair, grabbed the microphone, and began to perform. I twisted, I turned, I told moving stories, I made some powerful points. As I moved into the final act, I gave it all I had. With my last thought, I raised my hands and said, "Celebrate, celebrate!" I didn't get to finish the last line because a deafening roar filled my ears as the crowd rose with thunderous applause and loud cheers.

The day was a success. As I drove home, I reflected on the celebration. Why had it been such a success? I decided that these people had something important to celebrate: their successes. They were willing to take a risk—they dared to be different. Most important, they knew their hard efforts would pay off. Everyone was invited to the celebration and made to feel important.

Effective teams know there are many tools for inspiring individuals. They are sure to have a healthy blend of extrinsic and intrinsic rewards. Celebrations are designed around team members' belongingness needs, esteem needs, and self-actualization needs. This opens the door to an unlimited array of celebrations. Some team members respond to celebrations where there is food. Some respond to applause or any type of recognition. Some only need a compliment to keep them going. The key to all of this is for team members to know each other well and to develop celebrations that are really celebrations and not feeble attempts to do something for the sake of doing something.

Effective teams know how to make celebrations happen. They have spent team time talking about what they think is important to celebrate. The team members do not compete against each other. The only comparison they make is to themselves. They celebrate regularly and promptly. They do not recognize and celebrate inferior performance.

This chapter focuses on many different types of celebrations. It is included in the book because if teaming is the vehicle your organization is going to use to transform itself, it must be a vehicle that is in good working order. One way to keep it in working order is to recognize achievement, so the team will concentrate on images of itself succeeding. Success seems to have a profound effect on performance.

SIMPLE THINGS TO DO:
CELEBRATION—COME ON!

It's not the lofty sails but the unseen wind that moves the ship.

—W. Macneile Dixon

Background

A few years ago I received a call from the superintendent of a small county in North Carolina. He wanted to do something special for his entire staff to celebrate all the hard work its members had done to improve their school system. I suggested the theme School Should Be the Best Party in Town. I left it in his hands.

When I arrived to do the keynote, I was stunned. For a moment I thought I had stepped into Mardi Gras. The school was decorated to the hilt. Balloons were everywhere. The tables were decorated with confetti, party bags, and hand-painted signs. You name it, it was there. The superintendent was so excited. He handed me the letter he had sent to all the teachers. It told them to sleep in, and then at 9:00am they were to join the superintendent and school board for a celebration.

We began the morning of celebration with a band whose musicians were teachers. The superintendent asked us all to stand up and join him in a dance. He made a short speech about all their accomplishments and how proud they should be. The next thing I knew, 500 people were on their feet as the superintendent said, "Let's begin this new year by sliding into excellence." With that, the band started playing "The Electric Slide" and we all began to dance, the superintendent in the lead. As we laughed our way through the dance, each school came forward and did a cheer, each one better than the next. The enthusiasm was so powerful I began to cry. I know that sounds silly, but I was so touched by the sincere pride the superintendent felt toward his staff.

The rest of the day is another story that's better than this one, but I think I've made my point. Celebrations are important. They send the message that people are important. They uplift spirits and create a feeling of oneness. They boost morale. People laugh and share the accomplishment of common goals. Celebrations can be wonderful culminations of successful team work.

Did You Know

- Celebration serves as an important vehicle for informal communication and mingling across groups.
- Celebration provides opportunities for employees to develop a spirit of oneness.
- Celebration communicates a message that the organization cares about employees.
- People want to know their work matters.

#113. Things We Have/Haven't Done

You can do this activity every month or two. Get a large piece of paper and make three columns. The first column is headed Great Things We Have Done as a Team! The second column is Things We Have Done We *Never* Want to Do Again! The third column is Things We Haven't Done That We Want to Do! Ask the team members to brainstorm points under each column. When they're finished, decide together how they are going to celebrate Column 1.

Great Things We Have Done as a Team!	Things We Have Done We Never Want to Do Again!	Things We Haven't Done That We Want to Do!

Materials You Will Need

1 large chart with the three columns mentioned in this activity

a colored marker

masking tape

#114. Quick and Easy

Here are some ideas for celebrating at the end of each team meeting.

Silent Cheer—Ask someone to share something the team has done well. All team members raise their hands above their heads and shake them in a silent cheer.

Standing O—Ask each team member to stand and share one good thing that happened during the team meeting. After each member has shared, tell everyone to make an O with their hands. Then say, "You have just received your first standing ovation for a job well done."

Body Signs—Ask each person to share one good thing that happened at the team meeting. After each has shared, ask the team to come up with a body sign that represents the good things shared. An example might be a thumbs-up sign.

Back Rub—Share two or three things that made the meeting successful. Then ask all the team members to stand in a line facing to the right. Each member places his or her hands on the shoulders of the person ahead and, on the count of three, massages that person's shoulders. After a minute, members turn and face the opposite direction and massage again.

Materials You Will Need

#115. Graffiti Board

Designate a graffiti chart or board for the team. During the last five minutes of the meeting, encourage everyone to go to the board and write a word or a message that describes something the team did well during the meeting. Leave the comments up for the next couple of meetings.

LISTENED!

Took Turns

Brain Stormed

Focused!

Materials You Will Need

    graffiti board

    assorted colored markers

#116. Let's Party

Once every two months invite another team to join you for an after-work, 30-minute celebration party. Ask each team to share 5 to 10 things that happened in their team meetings that call for a celebration.

Materials You Will Need

refreshments or any other materials as desired

#117. Teammate of the Month

The team sets up criteria for this honor. At the last meeting of each month, the team votes on the teammate of the month. The teammate of the month award is one free lunch, one free favor, or whatever the team decides is an appropriate reward.

Materials You Will Need

whatever the team decides the award should be

THINGS THAT TAKE EFFORT: YOU'RE MY SOUL AND MY INSPIRATION

The greatest humiliation in life is to work hard on something from which you expect great appreciation, and then fail to get it.

—Edgar Watson Howe

Background

One time I worked with a team that had a really big and stressful project to do. We worked day and night. The project required a lot of cross-departmental cooperation, and we worked for months with no letup. Tempers were starting to fray, fatigue was setting in, and we began to wonder if we would ever get the project completed.

One day while sitting in my office, it suddenly dawned on me that we were getting too wrapped up in the project. We were no longer having fun! I picked up the phone and called all the team members. I told them I was declaring Friday a Swap, Buy, and Sell day. All the members were to meet in my office. They were to bring something from home they would like to swap or trade. We were going to have some fun. At first almost everyone was reluctant. After all, we were going to take work time to play. Somehow I persuaded them to do it anyway.

Friday arrived. We all met in my office. All the members laid out their items, and the Swap, Buy, and Sell began. It was absolutely hilarious. The funniest part was when individuals felt they had to give a sales pitch for why someone should buy their articles. We laughed until tears rolled down our faces. When the last item was gone, we closed our party with each person telling one thing about the project that he or she wanted to swap, buy, or sell to another teammate. Again, this brought much laughter. Needless to say, we worked toward the completion of the project with renewed vigor and enthusiasm. My old teammates still talk about Swap, Buy, and Sell.

Did You Know

- Play and fun in the workplace bond people together, reduce conflict, and create new visions.
- Without expressive events, any team will die.
- In a strong team, nothing is too trivial to celebrate.
- A team must celebrate if it's going to thrive.
- Celebrate the inches, because they lead to the touchdown.

#118. Sing a Song

Have the team develop an ad, cheer, song, or story that celebrates its successes. Have the members present their creation at a staff meeting or to other teams.

Materials You Will Need

the ad, cheer, song, or story from each team

refreshments if appropriate

#119. Spotlight Team of the Month

Each month, put a team in the spotlight. Ask the team members to have a team picture taken and put it on a bulletin board. Have them list what their accomplishments are. Give them reserved parking spaces near the building for the month. If the team meets every week, give the members a "meeting off" pass to use once during the month.

Materials You Will Need

team picture

reserved sign

team "meeting-off" pass

#120. Top Performance

Ask the entire organization to help develop some top performance awards. There is no limit to how many can be given out. If a team meets the criteria, it gets the award. If all the teams meet the criteria, all the teams are rewarded. Using the guidelines below, develop criteria and share them with the staff.

1. Determine what important things about teaming need to be rewarded.

2. Sell the program. The staff must believe in the recognition program and see that it is administered fairly.

3. Emphasize that this is not a competition or popularity contest.

4. Be careful when establishing criteria for award winners. The criteria must be as objective as possible.

5. Recognize winners regularly and promptly.

6. Do not recognize inferior performance. If there is no winner in a particular category, then don't give the award.

Materials You Will Need

whatever you and the teams decide will make good awards

FOR THE COMMITTED: TWIST AND SHOUT!

Don't be afraid to give your best to what seemingly are small jobs. Every time you conquer one, it makes you that much stronger. If you do little jobs well, the big ones tend to take care of themselves.

—Dale Carnegie

Background

I once attended an Institute for the Development of Educational Activities (IDEA) conference. It was the best conference experience of my life. When I arrived, I received a color-coded name tag on a string to wear around my neck. The colors represented the number of years a participant had attended the conference, and everyone was required to wear the neck tag all week. The upperclassmen were in charge of taking care of the lowerclassmen. On Wednesday night there was a talent show in which participants were highly encouraged to participate. The last day of the conference was graduation, and the conference planners made a big deal out of it. When a name was called out, people cheered and celebrated. Everyone I have met who has participated in this type of conference loves the IDEA group.

Why? Because it models what the research says about rituals and celebrations. The leaders know the impact these things have on people. Every year people return because they feel a sense of specialness—a sense of being valued as a person.

Did You Know

- Achievement deserves recognition.
- Recognition motivates higher accomplishments.
- The best-run organizations always make sure everyone understands why someone gets a reward.
- People have a way of becoming what you encourage them to be.
- Success stories have a significant ability to motivate people.
- When we see others succeed, it gives us hope that we can do it too.
- Most people are starved for appreciation.

#121. The Best Award Ever

This activity will take two to three hours to complete. It is only for the committed.

1. Ask the team members to talk about ceremonies they have seen or heard about that they thought were great. This sets the stage. It gets team members' creative juices flowing.

2. Distribute a stack of index cards to the team members and ask them to brainstorm as many types of awards and ceremonies as they can.

3. Have all members mark their two best ideas for a team award. Then go around the circle and ask each person to share his or her first choice. Tape each card on the wall. Next, have the members share their second choices. Then ask them to look at the rest of their cards and add any others they think should be included.

4. Have the team look at all the cards on the wall and remove any duplicates. Next, the recorder selects the first card on the list and asks the group if any of the other cards could go with this card. For example, if the first card was "Food," any card that had to do with food would go under this card. What you are doing here is grouping similar items.

5. Have each of the team members select a partner. Each pair takes one of the categories and writes a few sentences that pull all the information on the cards together. For example, if the category is "Food" and the cards under it are "Luncheon," "Cocktail party," and "A free lunch," one might write, "One of the awards we are considering involves food such as a free lunch, a cocktail party, or a team luncheon." Once this has been done, the partners develop a pro and con list for this type of award. After each category has been developed with pros and cons, the team meets to share the data. Each pair of partners shares its information with the team. After everyone has presented, the team decides which awards would be appropriate for their team.

6. The next step is to develop an action plan that includes criteria for the award, planning for the development of the award, evaluation of the award, and anything else the team deems necessary to make the ceremony a success.

Materials You Will Need

100 4 × 6 index cards

assorted colored markers

masking tape

chart paper

#122. Everyone's Involved

The entire organization may want to plan an awards ceremony for all the teams. If so, ask each team to select one team member to represent its team. This team member will serve on the award development team. Use the process outlined in Activity #121 and plan the awards ceremony for the entire organization.

Materials You Will Need

100 4 × 6 index cards

assorted colored markers

masking tape

chart paper

awards of the team's choice

11

Resisters You Will See

Organizations are full of all types of people. Some are team players and some are not. Some are happy and some are not. Some people like activities and some do not. This section of the book introduces you to some of the people you will meet and offers a suggestion or two that will help make the activities a success.

"I Don't Play"

These people are in every group. You will recognize them by their comments and body language. You will hear them comment under their breath (loud enough for you to hear), "I can't believe we're going to cut and paste. I don't have time for this." They have their arms crossed and a frown on their face.

The best way to deal with this is to take a proactive approach. At the beginning of the training, tell your audience that active participation is a very powerful way of learning. Tell them that all the activities require thinking and doing. Let them know that this is serious but at the same time fun. Invite them to participate. If you have some people who still resist, just leave them alone. I have learned that force never works. Everyone is accountable. Your job is to know the activity, use the best learning techniques you know, and put individuals in charge of their own learning. Most important, do not allow yourself to be intimidated.

"I'M AN INTROVERT"

At least a fourth of your audience will be introverted. People who are introverted would rather do things alone. They get their energy from within. At times people annoy them. You'll recognize the introverts because often they'll enter the room and sit by themselves. If they can't sit alone, they'll find other introverts. They get irritated when people talk when they're supposed to be working. When called upon, they may say, "Could you give me a minute to think?"

The best way to deal with introverts is to understand them. They are great people. They like to reflect and will do some of the best thinking in the group if they are allowed to. Since you know you'll have introverts, plan ahead. During the training, allow think time. Give people one- or two-minute warnings before you call time. Allow enough time to complete the activity. You might state at the beginning of the training that active participation is required and that you will provide reflection time.

"I'M UNCOMMITTED"

These people are often in the training because someone told them they had to attend. I have conducted workshops in which individuals had no idea why they were there. It's hard to be committed when you don't know why you're there! The uncommitted are easy to spot. They sit in the back, and often they'll let out little bark-like laughs when you give them directions for activities. They might try to intimidate you by staring a hole through you or wearing a smirk. The most intimidating are the ones who read the newspaper or clip their nails while you're talking.

My first suggestion is to breathe deeply and keep going. The most important thing is to know there will be one or two in the audience and to plan for them. When you open the session, be sure to give reasons why the training is important. The hope is that you can touch on something that will help them see what's in it for them. If that doesn't work, talk to them during a break. Find out something about them. Use them as examples. You might say, "Fred told me he's a math teacher. Let me give an example of how this can help math teachers." If none of this works, just ignore the person. This is hard to do, but as long as he or she is not bothering anyone, it may be the only thing you can do.

"I Know It All"

Every group has a know-it-all or two. There are two types. One type is the individual who thinks he or she knows everything there is to know about the topic. You'll recognize these people because they'll constantly interrupt you, they'll talk when you're talking, or they'll try their best to do the training for you. Then there are the types who have done this specific topic before. They've heard someone talking about the topic in the past, or they've read a book, or they went to a 30-minute work-shop and feel they don't need to know more or hear it again.

It's important for you to know which type of know-it-all a person is, because the techniques for dealing with the situation are different. If you find you have the first type, you must get on top of it quickly. First, acknowledge know-it-alls and thank them for sharing. After the third interruption, tell them you appreciate their knowledge and you will talk to them at the break. If that doesn't work, tell them you're trying to stick to a schedule and that perhaps they would like to help you with a follow-up session. Maybe they could reproduce some of their knowledge and give it to the group. When you see their hands go up, don't feel compelled to call on them. If nothing seems to work, see them at a break and ask them nicely not to interrupt. This takes some nerve, but these people are persistent and they'll get over it.

If you have the second type of know-it-all, one of the best techniques is to tell the group at the beginning that you realize there are all levels of knowledge in the room. Some people will hear something and say, "I know that!" Tell those people that perhaps they could be thinking of different ways to use the information in their lives. Also tell them that if they have information that is important and that you haven't mentioned, you would appreciate their sharing it with the group. You might also tell them that often we have to hear information a couple of times before it becomes powerful or useful. Another technique is to give lots of examples of how to use the information. The main point is to help this type of person see the information in another light.

"I'm Passive"

Bruce Joyce (1982), in his work on different types of learners, says that a large portion of an audience is passive. By that he means that these individuals are swayed by the people around them. They have enough energy to wonder about possibilities but don't get actively involved in pursuing options. You'll recognize them because they don't ever seem to get excited. They may be stallers who are hesitant, neutral, and indecisive. Worse yet, they can be unresponsive, noncommittal, and evasive. You may be doing your most rousing part of the training and look out and see a passive learner with a deadpan look on his or her face. All of a sudden your confidence begins to ebb.

These people are not harmful. They have no hidden agenda. They just don't get excited. Your best approach is to see if you can change the seating and get them next to someone who *does* get excited. A technique I have used is to tell the group to move around. Ask everyone to sit next to someone they haven't had an opportunity to talk to. It doesn't always work, but it's worth a try. It's also important for you to help the passive member see how the training relates to him or her. Above all, don't become discouraged, keep a positive outlook, and be sure you have a high energy level for what you're doing.

"What's in This for Me?"

These people enter the room with a glint in their eye and the question, "So, now what?" forming on their lips. They have that "show me" attitude.

One suggestion for dealing with this type of person is to be sure you state the purpose of the training up front. You might even say, "Let me tell you what is in this training for you." It will be important for you to get them to participate and contribute ideas. Expand on the benefits of the training.

"I'm Here to Be Seen"

These people are in a class all by themselves—and class is uppermost in their minds. They want to impress others, to "look good" in someone else's eyes. You'll recognize them because they will sit up front and volunteer for everything. They'll be involved, but it may be at a low level. In other words, they'll do the activities but they may not be involved at a high level. They may be the ones who finish within five minutes. You know in your heart they could not possibly have learned what you wanted them to learn.

These people are not hard to work with, because all you have to do is let them be seen and heard. Call on them, let them lead the group for a while, and talk to them on breaks. Notice them!

"I'm a Lifelong Learner"

I've left the best for last. We wish everyone could be like these people. They are there to learn. They are excited about the activities. They are thinking ahead to how they can use the information in their lives. They will take any and every opportunity to learn or refine an existing skill. You'll recognize them because they'll sit up front with a smile on their face and even yell "Right on!" during the training. They'll want copies of everything you have.

The best way to appeal to these people is to be sure you're interesting, well organized, and on target. Then say a little prayer of thanks that these people are in your training, because they make whatever other people you have to deal with worth it.

As I said earlier, some people are team players and some are not. Some like activities and some do not. The good news is that most people are absolutely delightful. I have found that when you treat people with dignity, they will do any activity you ask them to do, because people in organizations want to make a difference. That's what teaming is all about.

Final Note

*L*ike many others who have put their thoughts on paper, I have come to realize that there are stages to writing a book. These stages apply to any creative effort, including building teams. (I have borrowed the terminology from my business and industry friends. The characteristics under each are my own.)

The first stage is uninformed optimism. It is characterized by the following thoughts:

"I know I can do it!"

"I have a thousand and one ideas."

"I have something of value."

"I can't wait to begin."

"This is going to be easy."

It doesn't take long to get through this stage. After the first week, the truth sets in, and you immediately move into the second stage, informed pessimism. The reality of your commitment compared to your talents hits you in the face. This stage is characterized by the following thoughts:

"I don't think I have any original ideas."

"I can't do it."

"What if I fail?"

"Maybe I'll hide out in a foreign country."

The amount of time you spend in this stage depends upon your inner strength and your belief in effort versus luck. I stayed in this stage off and on for a month or so. Then with much effort I moved to Stage 3, hopeful realism. This stage is characterized by the following thoughts:

"Calm yourself—you can do it!"

"Oh, why not develop a plan?"

"Take some small steps. It's the inches that count!"

"Look at how much you have done. Go for it!"

This stage is what I call the light at the end of the tunnel. You know you'll make it, even if it takes months. It does! As you pass from this stage into the last stage, called successful completion, you begin to get excited as you send your last rewrite to the publisher or your team accomplishes its first goal. You breathe a sigh of relief and find this stage characterized by the following thoughts:

"It wasn't so hard."

"I did it, I did it!"

"I've forgotten the pain. I can't even remember I was ever afraid."

"I could do this forever."

As this stage draws to a close, you turn your thoughts to the future—what's next?

Further Readings

Atkinson, P. (1990). *Creating culture change: The key to successful total quality management.* San Diego, CA: Pfeiffer.

Bellanca, J., & Fogarty, R. (1991). *Blueprints for thinking in the cooperative classroom.* Thousand Oaks, CA: Corwin Press.

Bennis, W. (1989). *On becoming a leader.* Reading, MA: Addison-Wesley.

Block, P. (1987). *The empowered manager: Positive political skills at work.* San Francisco: Jossey-Bass.

Bormann, E., & Bormann, N. (1988). *Effective small group communication: Strategies and skills.* Edina, MN: Burgess.

Brassard, M., & Ritter, D. (1994). *The Memory Jogger™ II.* Salem, NH: GOAL/QPC.

Costa, A., & Garmston, R. (1986). *The art of cognitive coaching: Supervision for intelligent teaching.* El Dorado Hills, CA: Institute for Intelligent Behavior.

Covey, S. (1989). *The 7 habits of highly effective people.* New York: Simon & Schuster.

Darling-Hammond, L. (1996). What matters most: A competent teacher for every child. *Phi Delta Kappan, 78*(3), 193–200.

Deal, T., & Kennedy, A. (1982). *Corporate cultures: The rites and rituals of corporate life.* Reading, MA: Addison-Wesley.

Deming, W. E. (2000). *Out of the crisis.* Cambridge, MA: MIT Press.

Doyle, M., & Straus, D. (1976). *How to make meetings work: The new interaction method.* New York: Wyden Books.

DuFour, R., & Eaker, R. (1998). *Professional learning communities at work: Best practices for enhancing student achievement.* Bloomington, IN: National Educational Service.

Eaker, R., DuFour, R., & Burnette, R. (2002). *Getting started: Reculturing schools to become professional learning communities.* Bloomington, IN: National Educational Service.

Feder, M. (1989). *Taking charge.* Mission, KS: SkillPath.

Forte, I., & Schurr, S. (2002). *The definitive middle school guide: A handbook for success* (Rev. ed.). Nashville, TN: Incentive.

Francis, D., & Young, D. (1979). *Improving work groups: A practical manual for team building.* San Diego, CA: Pfeiffer.

Fullan, M. (1993). *Change forces: Probing the depths of educational reform.* London: Falmer Press.

Garfield, C. (1986). *Peak performers: The new heroes of American business.* New York: William Morrow.

Glanz, J. (2006). *What every principal should know about collaborative leadership.* Thousand Oaks, CA: Corwin Press.

Glickman, C. (2003). *Holding sacred ground: Essays on leadership, courage, and endurance in our schools.* San Francisco: Jossey-Bass.

Hackett, D., & Martin C. (1993). *Facilitation skills for team leaders.* Boston: Course Technology.

Hickman, C., & Silva, M. (1984). *Creating excellence: Managing corporate culture, strategy, and change in the new age.* New York: New American Library.

Hunter, M. (1976). *Improved instruction.* Thousand Oaks, CA: Corwin Press.

Jackson, A., & Davis, G. (2000). *Turning points 2000: Educating adolescents in the 21st century.* New York: Teachers College Press.

Jacobs, E., Harvill, R., & Masson, R. (2006). *Group counseling: Strategies and skills* (5th ed.). Belmont, CA: Thomson/Brooks/Cole.

Johnson, D., & Johnson, R. (1994). *Leading the cooperative school* (2nd ed.). Edina, MN: Interaction Books.

Joyce, B. (1982). [Untitled]. Paper presented at Henrico Public School Systems, Henrico County, VA.

Kagan, S. (1994). *Cooperative learning.* San Clemente, CA: Kagan Cooperative Learning.

Kolb, D., Rubin, I., & McIntrye, J. (Eds.). (1984). *Organizational psychology: An experiential approach* (4th ed.). Englewood Cliffs, NJ: Prentice Hall.

Lambert, L. (2003). *Leadership capacity for lasting school improvement.* Alexandria, VA: Association for Supervision and Curriculum Development.

Lazear, D. (1999). *Eight ways of knowing* (3rd ed.). Thousand Oaks, CA: Corwin Press.

Maddux, R., & Wingfield, B. (2003). *Team building: An exercise in leadership* (4th ed.). Menlo Park, CA: Crisp Learning.

Martinez, M. (2004). *Teachers working together for school success.* Thousand Oaks, CA: Corwin Press.

Marzano, R. (2001). *Classroom instruction that works.* Alexandria, VA: Association for Supervision and Curriculum Development.

Marzano, R., Waters, T., & McNulty, B. (2005). *School leadership that works: From research to results.* Alexandria, VA: Association for Supervision and Curriculum Development.

Maxwell, J. (2003). *The 17 indisputable laws of teamwork workbook.* Nashville, TN: Thomas Nelson.

McGinnis, A. (1985). *Bringing out the best in people.* Minneapolis, MN: Augsburg.

Parker, G. (1990). *Team players and teamwork: The new competitive business strategy.* San Francisco: Jossey-Bass.

Peck, M. S. (1987). *The different drum: Community-making and peace.* New York: Simon & Schuster.

Phillips, S., & Elledge, R. (1989). *The team-building source book.* San Diego, CA: University Associates.

Quinlivan-Hall, D., & Renner, P. (1994). *In search of solutions: 60 Ways to guide your problem-solving group.* San Diego, CA: Pfeiffer.

Roberts, S., & Pruitt, E. (2003). *Schools as professional learning communities: Collaborative activities and strategies for professional development.* Thousand Oaks, CA: Corwin Press.

Schmoker, M. (2001). *The results field book.* Alexandria, VA: Association for Supervision and Curriculum Development.

Scholtes, P., Joiner, B., & Streibel, B. (2003). *The TEAM handbook* (3rd ed.). Madison, WI: Oriel.

Schwarz, R. (1994). *The skilled facilitator.* San Francisco: Jossey-Bass.

Secretary's Commission on Achieving Necessary Skills. (1991). *SCANS Report.* Washington, DC: U.S. Department of Labor.

Senge, P. (1990). *The fifth discipline: The art and practice of the learning organization.* New York: Doubleday.

Sheehan, M. (1992). *Good advice.* New York: Wing Books.

Silberman, M. (1999). *101 ways to make meetings active.* San Francisco: Jossey-Bass/Pfeiffer.

Streibel, B. (2003). *The manager's guide to effective meetings.* Chicago: McGraw-Hill.

Torp, L., & Sage, S. (2002). *Problems as possibilities* (2nd ed.). Alexandria, VA: Association for Supervision and Curriculum Development.

Tuckman, B. (1965). Developmental sequence in small groups. *Psychological Bulletin, 63*(6), 384–399.

Varney, G. (1989). *Building productive teams: An action guide and resource book.* San Francisco: Jossey-Bass.

Vogt, J., & Murrell, K. (1990). *Empowerment in organizations: How to spark exceptional performance.* San Diego, CA: Pfeiffer.

Walton, M. (1986). *The Deming management method.* New York: Putnam.

Ziglar, Z. (2003). *Top performance: How to develop excellence in yourself and others* (Rev. ed.). Grand Rapids, MI: F. H. Revell.

Index